UNDERSTANDING NORTHERN IRELAND

UNDERSTANDING NORTHERN IRELAND

DERMOT QUINN

baseline
BOOKS

First published 1993 by
Baseline Book Company
PO Box 34
Chorlton
Manchester M21 1LL

British Library Cataloguing in Publication Data

ISBN 1 897626 03 7

Cover design   Ian Price
Cover illustration   Min Cooper
Typesetting   Kathryn Holliday
Printed and bound by Nuffield Press, Oxford

ACKNOWLEDGEMENTS

I should like to thank Paul and Archy Quinn for help in compiling statistics, Ian Holliday for editorial suggestions, and Mary Burke for literary advice. The book's faults belong to the author. **DQ**

CONTENTS

TABLES

ABBREVIATIONS

DUP	Democratic Unionist Party
IDB	Industrial Development Board
IRA	Irish Republican Army
LEDU	Local Enterprise Development Unit
NICRA	Northern Ireland Civil Rights Association
NIHE	Northern Ireland Housing Executive
Noraid	Northern Aid Committee
OUP	Ulster ('Official') Unionist Party
RUC	Royal Ulster Constabulary
SDLP	Social Democratic and Labour Party
UDA	Ulster Defence Association
UDR	Ulster Defence Regiment
UPNI	Unionist Party of Northern Ireland
UUUC	United Ulster Unionist Council
UVF	Ulster Volunteer Force
UWC	Ulster Workers Council

INTRODUCTION

The distinctiveness of Ulster – within both Ireland and the United Kingdom – is a matter of record. The significance of that distinctiveness is a matter of debate. Ulster has for centuries been different, a 'place apart'. Now, as Europe moves towards *de facto* federalism, its oddity appears all the more marked: sectarian in politics in an age of pluralism and self-absorbed in an age of widening vistas. Communism has been and gone; the nation-state has had its day. Only at the extremities of Europe – Ulster to the northwest, Bosnia to the southeast – does extremism still reign. As the twenty-first century beckons, Northern Ireland seems content to remain in the seventeenth.

THE BURDEN OF HISTORY

This book attempts to explain the Northern Ireland conflict. More than any other problem of contemporary British politics, its roots are ancient. The opening chapters of this book therefore provide necessary historical context.

Chapter 1 shows that from at least as early as the seventeenth century north-eastern Ireland was different from the rest of the country. Chapter 2 describes the crucial period 1920-72, when Northern Ireland's parliament failed to win support from all of the province's citizens. In a context of mounting civil strife, it was suspended by the Heath government in 1972. Since then, with one brief interlude, Northern Ireland has been ruled directly from Westminster.

Various initiatives have subsequently been attempted to bring peace. None has worked. Chapters 3 and 4 analyse them, from 'power-sharing' in 1974 to the Anglo-Irish Agreement in 1985, suggesting that each initiative was in some way flawed.

CONTEMPORARY POLITICS AND POLICY

The remainder of the book is more topical. Chapter 5 examines the workings of Thatcherism in Northern Ireland, seeking to determine the extent to which the full doctrine was applied and the impact it had there. Chapter 6 considers the changing identities of the political parties throughout the 'troubles'. Chapter 7 looks at Northern Ireland in an international context, and Chapter 8 analyses security, law and order, and the paramilitary culture.

Finally, in Chapters 9 and 10, there is a consideration of politics after 1985: unionist and nationalist responses to the Anglo-Irish Agreement, and the efforts of the British government to sustain talks to bring about a new form of administration for Northern Ireland. Some conclusions and a prediction are then offered.

HISTORY LESSONS

Paradoxes abound in Northern Ireland. One is the peacefulness of the place. No town or village has been unaffected, but for the most part violence has been localised. The motto might by 'Business as Usual'. Another peculiarity relates to the problem's persistence: the Northern Ireland question remains unsolved precisely because there are so many solutions to it. Punditry, academic or otherwise, has never been in short supply. Ireland has often been miraculously pacified after the third pint only to erupt again after the tenth. Nor is this a phenomenon of recent vintage. If history teaches any lessons, it is that the Irish problem has been solved over and over again. Henry VIII's answer was to extend the authority of the Crown. Elizabeth I thought – endearingly – that Trinity College, Dublin, would do the trick. Dr Johnson – more imaginative than most – suggested an exchange of populations of Ireland and Holland.

There is here, in other words, a lesson *about* history as much as from history. The liberal mind sometimes reposes excessive confidence in perspective, as if knowing the past can of itself resolve the problems of the present. That is rationalist naïvete. Understanding Northern Ireland is not the same as pacifying it: the opposite, perhaps. To recognise a riddle is not to solve it. Nor should the historian claim access to greater wisdom than others. The punditry of previous eras was often as cock-eyed as our own.

1 THE ROOTS OF THE NORTHERN IRELAND PROBLEM

The Northern Ireland problem has deep roots. It cannot be understood without reference to history. As early as the seventeenth century, a pattern was established which helps us make sense of Northern Ireland's current difficulties.

A PLACE APART

Prior to 1609, Ulster's distinctiveness lay in its remoteness. As the Tudors attempted to 'modernise' Ireland – that is, to make it more English – the north eastern part of the country remained most resistant to change. Physically, it was hilly, heavily wooded, unyieldingly bleak. Politically, it lay under the sway of Gaelic-speaking clans – the O'Neills, the O'Donnells, the O'Kanes – men with scant or merely pragmatic loyalty to the crown. In myriad ways, it mocked English claims to sovereignty: its religion was Catholic, its system of land inheritance tribal, its laws based on ancient codes of honour, its folk culture oral not written.

Under the Tudors, English policy in Ireland had been to bring the country under closer political, commercial and legal control. The results were mixed. The Protestant Reformation was introduced and legally enforced; a new land-holding policy was attempted; Gaelic lords were cultivated. For all that, Ireland remained untamed. A more dramatic policy was therefore undertaken: dispossession of the native peoples and recolonisation of their land by English settlers. This 'plantation' began in the province of Munster in the 1530s. The 'New English', as they were called, – military types, Protestants, risk-takers – steadily altered the topography and politics of their adoptive country, but the cost was high. The Gaelic clans who lost their lands never reconciled themselves to the new dispensation. Rebellion became an endemic feature of sixteenth-century Ireland. Its peculiar configuration – Gaelic Catholic backwardness versus English Protestant modernisation – has constituted, in different guises, the dichotomous dynamic of Irish history ever since.

Nowhere was this more apparent than in Ulster. By 1600, anglicisation had taken the usual forms, but had been met by increasingly powerful resistance. Central to this resistance was Hugh O'Neill, whom Elizabeth I had created Earl of Tyrone. O'Neill accepted English honours, but only as a way of strengthening his position as a Gaelic chieftain. He had no intention of submitting to the Crown, even though he had earlier fought on Elizabeth's behalf. At last, in 1598, he rose in rebellion to preserve, as he saw it, the Gaelic way of life in Ulster. He nearly succeeded, but ultimate victory proved elusive. He was defeated in 1601 and made submission to the Crown in 1603. Thereafter O'Neill was a spent force, and in 1607 he and his fellow rebel chieftains were forced into European exile.

PLANTATION

This 'flight of the earls' was an important moment in Irish history. English rule in Ulster had been chronically unstable. Now it was possible, the Gaelic lords gone, to attempt a far more systematic application of the policy of 'plantation'. The effects were dramatic. Gaelic rebels were declared forfeit of their land, which was then parcelled out in lots of varying sizes to English soldiers, merchants and entrepreneurs. These were people willing to resettle and take a risk, to enrich themselves and secure royal authority in an unruly place. They transformed the face of Ulster, clearing woods, draining land, establishing and fortifying towns, introducing Protestantism. Sober, industrious and 'loyal', they turned what had been the most Irish part of Ireland into the most 'English'.

For all that, Ulster did not become a replica England. The new settlers were self-consciously a garrison. They had been granted land on the understanding that they would defend it. Moreover, they were forbidden to consort with the native Irish – indication of the incompleteness of the dispossession. Their culture was alien, and they knew it. Nervously they tilled a soil not their own.

Another element demands mention. Look at a map and notice one of the most significant determinants of Ulster's history: proximity to Scotland. Well before the seventeenth century there had been a reasonably constant flow of Scottish settlers in the north east of Ireland. Under the Stuarts this stream became a torrent. To this immigration may be traced some of the peculiarities of speech, dialect, custom and accent which have remained characteristic of Ulster (especially eastern Ulster) to modern times. More than from England, Ulster was 'planted' from lowland Scotland: and when the native Irish turned surly it was to lowland Scotland that the settlers turned for support.

Yet even to speak of 'native Irish' is to beg two questions. In the first place, hybridity not homogeneity was the essence of pre-plantation Ireland. The plantation merely added strains – some English, some Scottish – to an already mixed population. Some were well aware of this at the time. In the second place, terms such as 'English', 'Scottish', 'Irish' cannot properly be used in a political sense in the seventeeth century. 'Nations', still less 'nation-states', had yet to emerge. Thus to speak of 'English' or 'Irish' is to make more of a geographical than political statement.[1]

Does this matter? It certainly weakens one of the narrower claims of Irish nationalism – that 'England' attempted to conquer 'Ireland' in the seventeeth century, and that a pure Gaelic people was dispossessed by English and Scots. Equally it should make us cautious in face of another claim which has gained ground recently: that there exists also a separate Ulster nationalism. This seems grandiose, as if a few easily caricatured attributes – bluntness of speech, thrift, a capacity for hard work – constitute nationhood. It is also quasi-racist, elevating Ulster 'stock' into the Ulster 'nation'. The racial grounds of either of Ireland's 'nationalisms' are hard to sustain.

NATIVE VERSUS PLANTER

None of this is to deny the reality of dispossession nor the anger it caused. Vengeance, when it came, was swift. Resentment exploded into rebellion in 1641 when many of the settlers were put to death by those whose lands they had expropriated. Contemporary accounts suggest extraordinary brutality – stripping, dismemberment, drowning, burning. Three hundred and fifty years later, Ulster Protestants have not forgotten it. They continue to count the corpses of 1641, aware of parallels with their own situation.

The Ulster rising sparked a general revolt of dispossessed Irish which lasted ten years. In a situation made yet more complex by Civil War in England, different armies took to the field, some proclaiming loyalty to Pope, others to Parliament, others to the Crown. Only when Oliver

Cromwell arrived in Ireland in 1649 was the issue resolved. With massive force he crushed the Catholic rebellion, claiming himself an instrument of civility as he did so. In the subsequent resettlement of Irish property, Catholics were punished severely. They were sent 'to Hell or Connacht' – Cromwell's grim phrase – meaning that many were forced into exile or to the poorest region of the country. By 1652, three-quarters of the land of Ireland was in the hands of a small minority of Protestants.

The Cromwellian settlement was never reversed, though some attempts were made to modify it. Catholics lived in hope of a restoration of their lands. With the accession of James II in 1685 it seemed as if their moment had come. James gave every sign of favouring Catholicism: in England, by easing restrictive legislation, in Ireland by opening the army and municipal offices to the former 'rebels'. Many Irish Protestants took alarm, fleeing to Holland to enlist in the army of William, Prince of Orange. English Protestants were also alarmed, and they too looked to William for support. In the 'Glorious Revolution' of 1688 William bloodlessly overthrew James. In 1689 he and his wife Mary (James's daughter) jointly acceded to the throne.

James was down but not out. Exiled in France but assured of solid Catholic support in Ireland, he gathered an army, hoping to secure Ireland before winning back his crown in England. He landed in Ireland to considerable acclaim. Catholics flocked to his colours in a final effort to win back their lands. But the cause was forlorn. William mustered a great army of his own and travelled to Ireland to face the pretender. The Pope (as ironists delight to record) supported Protestant William against Catholic James, the latter being the ally of Rome's enemy, France. In a series of confrontations – Derry, Aughrim, the Boyne – the Jacobites were routed, so that by 1691 Williamite Protestantism was triumphant in Ireland.

William is hero to many Ulster Protestants: 1690 means to them the victory of religious liberty and the defeat of popery. This may seem paradoxical, but it makes sense if Catholicism itself is considered the enemy of religious and political freedom. Whatever the truth of that, Catholicism was forced underground in Ireland after William's victory: bishops sent into exile, priests outlawed, the Mass prohibited, Catholic entry into the professions closed, land-holding made difficult. For most of the eighteenth century, Anglicanism was the denomination of the political and social establishment in Ireland. Here, however, is a genuine paradox: the Williamite victory did not necessarily favour all the Protestants of Ulster. Many dissenters, of Scots Presbyterian stock, also suffered legal disabilities after 1691. They formed no part of the 'Protestant Ascendancy', which was strictly Anglican. It is ironic that the modern day Orangeman should be so ardent in his enthusiasm for a victory which stifled even the dissenting tradition.

EIGHTEENTH-CENTURY IRELAND

Irish Protestants developed a distinctive political identity in the eighteenth century. They came to see themselves not as the 'English in Ireland' but as the Irish nation itself. Here was not an outpost to be colonised but a land they were proud to call their own. Protestant patriotism reached an apogee in 1782 when Ireland won 'Legislative Independence' from England. This meant the Irish House of Commons (hitherto weak) could now initiate legislation on its own account without having to wait for Westminster to act. It did not mean that Ireland was independent of England. Irish patriots such as Henry Grattan, the architect of victory, could now plausibly claim that Ireland and England were separate nations sharing a Crown but not a parliament.

The euphoria produced by this constitutional revolution proved short-lived. 'Grattan's Parliament' was weak, unrepresentative, and incapable of self-reform. Catholics were excluded from it. Nor had it an answer for the sectarian violence which from the 1780s had become endemic in the Irish countryside. The outbreak of the French Revolution sounded its death-knell. Just as the American Revolution had encouraged the demand for legislative independence, so the French Revolution prompted a radical republicanism which sought complete separation. This was powerfully articulated by the United Irish Society under the leadership of the Protestant lawyer Theobald Wolfe Tone. The Society was founded in Belfast and drew heavily on the Ulster radical tradition which stressed political and individual liberty for all, Dissenter and Catholic alike. Tone was an idealistic non-sectarian: he believed that it was only by Irishmen of all faiths coming together that the connection between England and Ireland – 'the never failing source of all our political evils' – might be broken.

There was simplicity and clarity to this anti-Englishness; versatility, too. Tone, as he plotted revolution after 1795, believed that opposition to England could unite his countrymen as nothing else. But the analysis was partial. Irishmen were *not* united. They were bitterly divided by religion. In the north, secret societies such as the (Catholic) Defenders and the (Protestant) Peep O'Day Boys engaged in rural terrorism to protect against the perceived economic threat of the Catholic peasantry to the Protestant and vice versa. Nor had memories dimmed of dispossession and of massacre. Tone's movement had appeal in radical, middle-class Belfast, in parts of Antrim and Down, but none in places such as Armagh where the balance of Catholic to Protestant was roughly equal and each regarded the other warily.

The rebellion of 1798 was supposed to sever the English connection with Ireland, but it proved a bloody fiasco. It was badly planned, French assistance came too late, and the government (through an elaborate network of informers) knew of it well in advance. Worse, insurrection simply became a cover for settling old sectarian scores. In counties Armagh and Wexford Catholic and Protestant massacred one another with appalling relish. Human butchery became commonplace, hanging and 'piking' to death a casual occurrence. The year of the rising saw perhaps 30 000 violent deaths in Ireland.

The country was plainly incapable of self-government. An Act of Union was passed in 1800 which abolished 'Grattan's Parliament' and transferred Irish political representation (still exclusively Protestant) to Westminster. Who supported this Union? Many Catholics did, making them the first 'unionists'. Many Protestants opposed, making them 'nationalists'. For all that, the Union divided Ireland less along sectarian than economic lines. In Ulster, for example, the chief consideration was the impact on the linen trade, some merchants thinking that union would promote it, others disagreeing. Elsewhere, predictable vested interests expressed themselves: Dubliners disliked the loss of their parliament, people in the regions hoped for improved trade with England, the Catholic gentry tended to favour the union, the Catholic peasantry were indifferent.

IRELAND UNDER THE UNION

Two Irelands gradually emerged under this Union, divisible by region, social class and political predilection. On the one hand was Ulster: prosperous, mainly protestant, much enhanced by the English connection. An incipient industrial revolution took hold in the early nineteenth century. Belfast became a major port and centre of manufacturing. Many Catholics came to live there from the south and west of the province, boosting their share of the population from 5 per cent in 1800 to 35 per cent in 1850. They settled mainly in the west of the city, an alien presence among the Protestant working classes whose territory they seemed to supplant.

As trade with Britain flourished, so also did the conviction that prosperity, Protestantism and the Union were the reasons. Indeed, this belief became a powerful axiom for many nineteenth-century Ulstermen: their twentieth-century counterparts have often argued similarly. Yet if Ulster was prosperous it was not always peaceful. Sectarian disturbance was a prominent feature of its social landscape, with serious riots in Belfast in 1857, 1864 and 1886, in Derry in 1869 and 1883. Any number of factors could spark trouble: a parade, an ill-chosen speech, a local bullying. Tensions often ran high on 12 July, when the Orange Order celebrated William's victory over James at the Battle of the Boyne. But this was not the only source of trouble. Riot had its own ritual, a subtle pattern of provocation and response not easily reducible to a single cause. It was also perennial. Each generation seemed to learn anew the belligerent habits of its predecessor, one side fighting the other because it was the done thing.

SOUTHERN SORROWS

The Union thus reinforced, for good and ill, Ulster's status as a 'place apart'. The rest of Ireland fared less well. Before the great potato famine of 1845-51, popular opinion was mobilised for two causes: the right of Catholics to sit in the House of Commons, which succeeded, and repeal of the Union, which failed. Under the leadership of Daniel O'Connell (1775-1847), the Catholic peasantry and tenantry acquired a political consciousness, directed against British rule in Ireland. The Famine, in which between a million and a million and a half people died of starvation or disease, reinforced that alienation. Bitterness at England's apparent indifference to Ireland's suffering ran deep, making the demand for self-government more insistent.

The growth of physical force nationalism was one expression of the popular mood. Militantly republican groups such as the Fenians emerged in the late 1850s, their aim to expel Britain from Ireland by force of arms. Fenianism was nothing short of an international conspiracy against British rule the world over. It flourished especially in the United States, where many Irishmen (fleeing from famine) had trained themselves in the Civil War to fight their nation's historic enemy. Fenianism's moment of glory came in 1867 when 80 000 men in England and Ireland planned to rise in insurrection. As was usually the case with Irish rebellions, this was more impressive in ambition than execution. Most of the action occurred around Dublin, Cork, Tipperary and Limerick in March. Great numbers on paper turned out to be phantoms, and the rising was easily crushed. But it had political significance: for the first time, English public opinion became aware of the 'Irish Question' and of the need, in Gladstone's phrase, 'to pacify Ireland'.

During Gladstone's first ministry (1868-74) various attempts were made to cure the disease of which the Fenian rising was the most dramatic symptom. The Church of Ireland was disestablished, Irish land law was modestly reformed to favour tenant rights, an effort was made, ultimately unsuccessful, to provide state-funded university education for Catholics. These were well intentioned but in the end only encouraged a closer scrutiny of the constitutional relationship between England and Ireland. Many came to believe that Ireland needed not palliatives but a parliament of her own. The emergence in the late 1870s of a well organised 'Home Rule' party under Charles Stewart Parnell gave expression to the sentiment. Parnell combined formidable tactical and procedural skills with a powerful hold over the rural Catholic masses. He demanded a parliament in Dublin, which would remain nevertheless subordinate to the Westminster parliament. In 1886 his party held the balance of power at Westminster, and with Gladstone's conversion to Home Rule it looked as if Parnell might succeed.

It was not to be. Gladstone's party split on the matter, thus robbing him of his parliamentary majority. Home Rule failed in 1886. It failed again in 1893, when Gladstone, in office for the last time, was able to pass a measure through the Commons only to see it thrown out by the Lords. Nevertheless, these developments alarmed the Protestants of Ulster. As early as O'Connell's campaign for repeal of the Act of Union there had been awareness that Ulster's distinctiveness demanded special consideration. Sixty years on, little had changed. To Protestants, Home Rule meant Rome Rule – the swamping of their way of life under a Catholic-controlled parliament in Dublin. Gladstone had once been hero to many, especially liberal-minded Presbyterians. After 1886, he became villain. Protestant Liberalism died in Ulster that year, replaced by a unionism which appealed to all, regardless of class or social station.

All classes resisted. Their defiance was not bravado. Although the threat of Home Rule receded after 1893, Irish unionists, especially in the north, were not prepared to go quietly. 'Ulster will fight,' Lord Randolph Churchill famously asserted, 'and Ulster will be right'.

TOWARDS REVOLUTION

The reckoning did not come for another twenty years. In the interim Irish politics shifted radically. Home Rule at Westminster languished. Gladstone's double failure was a bitter blow to its supporters, who also had to contend with Parnell's loss of the party leadership following a divorce scandal, his early death, and the spilt of the Irish Nationalist party into Parnellites and anti-Parnellites. In 1895 the Conservatives resumed power, pledged to resist any breach in the union, pursuing instead a policy of 'killing Home Rule with kindness'.

In Ireland itself Home Rule lost its allure, not because it was too radical but because it was not radical enough. Some began to formulate national identity in terms not of Home Rule but of complete separation from England. This was the result of a powerful 'Gaelic Revival' which promoted all things Irish – language, ancient literature, folk-customs, games – and deplored most things English, including Home Rule. These cultural separatists perceived that Parnell's policy (even granting its success) would enshrine, not end, Irish national subordination. And there were nationalists of another school who gave priority to labour issues, rejecting Home Rule as the replacement of one set of bosses – English – by another – Irish. To James Connolly (1868-1916), founder of the Irish Socialist Republican Party in 1896, Ireland's relationship with England was a form of colonial subjection which had to be broken before socialism could be achieved.

By 1910, then, it looked as if Home Rule would not be enough for some. It was of course too much for Ulster. For all that, it remained the presumed desire of a majority of the people of Ireland. Moreover, it looked as if it could no longer be postponed. The Liberal Party had won power by a large margin in 1906 – large enough for them not to have to introduce a Home Rule bill to gain the support of the Irish Parliamentary Party. Two general elections in 1910 changed that.

Fighting on Lloyd George's controversial budget of 1909, the Liberals saw their majority virtually disappear. More than that, to pass the budget they had to break the resistance of the House of Lords. The Parliament Act 1911 ended the veto power of the second chamber. With that obstacle gone, there was nothing to prevent the passage of a Home Rule Bill. A measure was duly introduced in April 1912, receiving its third reading in the Commons in January 1913. It was only a matter of time before it would become law.

Protestant Ulster rose to this challenge. During and after passage of the bill, a series of mass meetings urged defiance. Support came from Conservative leader Andrew Bonar Law, who could imagine 'no length of resistance' which he would not be prepared to support. In September 1913 almost a quarter of a million men signed a 'Solemn League and Covenant' pledging to resist Home Rule even at the cost of their lives. Military exercises took place, organised by the Ulster Volunteer Force (UVF). Arms and ammunition were secretly shipped by night: on 25 April 1914, for example, 24 000 rifles and three million rounds were smuggled into Bangor and Larne.

As Ulster armed, so did the rest of Ireland. Although the Home Rule Bill was destined to become law, nationalists feared that Ulster (or some part of it) might be excluded from its operations. The northern resistance had alarmed the government, and Prime Minister Asquith was prepared to buy peace. There was little the Nationalist Party could do to prevent exclusion of Ulster, because Asquith could rely on Tory support for any special treatment for the province. And so nationalists took their cue from unionists. Alarmed that the bill might be mutilated, many joined the 'Irish Volunteers', an analogue of the Ulster Volunteers. As Patrick Pearse, schoolmaster and future revolutionary, remarked, an Orangeman with a rifle was a less ridiculous figure than a nationalist without one. By summer 1914, Ireland had formed itself into two armed camps and civil war seemed imminent.

THE EASTER RISING

The outbreak of the First World War changed the situation. The third Home Rule bill, covering all of Ireland, was signed into law shortly after the war began; but its operation was suspended for twelve months or for the duration of the war, whichever proved longer. It was expected that an 'Amending Bill' might also be passed to exclude parts of Ulster, but nationalists did not take that prospect seriously. Many of them in fact joined the colours to fight, believing that demonstrations of loyalty would win for Ireland a full measure of Home Rule when the war was over.

Not all nationalists were loyal, however, or pleased with the passage of a Home Rule bill. When war broke out, the republican separatist tradition re-asserted itself. England's difficulty was Ireland's opportunity. A small coterie led by Patrick Pearse and James Connolly plotted a rising to secure complete independence for Ireland. Gaelic Leaguers, trades unionists, advanced socialists, old-style Fenians, they commanded little support when in Easter 1916 they proclaimed an Irish Republic. Claiming to speak 'in the name of God and of the dead generations', they spoke only for themselves. They held out for a week, but their rising was never more than a gesture. British artillery pounded them into submission, and they were booed through the streets of Dublin when they surrendered.

None the less in failure lay the seed of later triumph. The rebellion was not popular, but the execution of its leaders turned public opinion against Britain. Republicanism had a new set of martyrs, a new 'dead generation'. Thereafter Home Rule would never be sufficient to satisfy nationalist demands. In the 1918 election the Nationalist party went down to massive defeat at the hands of a new group, Sinn Fein, pledged to abstain from Westminster and to establish its own parliament in Dublin. Sinn Fein won nearly three-quarters of all seats, though few in Ulster, where unionism scored its usual triumph.

PARTITION

The Sinn Fein parliament (Dail Eireann) met for the first time in January 1919 and, with the swiftness of a curtain rising on a play, an Irish Republic seemed to be in place: Eamon de Valera its president, Michael Collins its finance minister, a host of other cabinet officers, all claiming political, legal and administrative jurisdiction over Ireland. This challenge to British authority was accompanied by violence, at first sporadic, then systematic – ambushing of policemen, attacks on military vehicles, shooting of informers – undertaken by the Irish Volunteers, who now styled themselves the Irish Republican Army (IRA). Britain's response came in the form of a special auxiliary force and English-recruited police reinforcements known colloquially (because of their uniforms) as the 'Black and Tans', who matched the IRA blow for blow. By the end of 1920 Ireland was in the grip of a war of independence, fought without quarter on either side.

In the thick of war and with its jurisdiction under assault, Britain now attempted to make good its 1914 promise to introduce a measure of Home Rule. This may seem strange, and the measure was hardly suited to the situation on the ground, but the attempt was itself an exercise of jurisdiction, a last effort to retrieve a lost cause. The Government of Ireland Act 1920 was Lloyd George's answer to the Ulster question and to the war of independence. Two parliaments were to be established, one for 'Southern Ireland', the other for 'Northern Ireland'. Both would have identical powers, and both would cede ultimate authority to the Westminster parliament, which reserved for itself control over defence, foreign affairs, direct taxation, and some smaller matters. 'Northern Ireland' was to consist of the six counties of Derry, Tyrone, Fermanagh, Antrim, Armagh and Down, 'Southern Ireland' of the remainder of the country. The proposal was controversial. It excluded from 'Northern Ireland' unionists who lived in the three remaining Ulster counties (Donegal, Cavan, Monaghan) and included nationalists who wished no part of it.

The Act held no appeal for southern nationalists, who remained loyal to the 'Irish Republic' and continued the war of independence much as before. For northern unionists it was a godsend. Initially suspicious, they came to see that partition represented the best guarantee of their way of life. Some would have preferred that all nine Ulster counties be included in Northern Ireland, but the unionist majority in such a unit would have been precarious. Accordingly, they set about making the Act a reality. Elections were held in May 1921, Unionists winning 40 of the 52 seats, Sinn Fein and Nationalists (on abstentionist tickets) the remaining 12. The Northern Ireland parliament was opened in Belfast in June 1921 by King George V, who made a plea for 'a new era of peace, contentment and goodwill'. He made no reference to the fact that those who had once been the strongest opponents of Home Rule were now its firmest supporters. Unionists, a minority in Ireland, had majority status thrust upon them in one part of it. Could they rise to the challenge of political maturity?

NOTE

1 cf. ATQ Stewart, *The Narrow Ground: The Roots of Conflict in Ulster* (Faber and Faber, London, 1989), pp40ff.

2 NORTHERN IRELAND 1921-72

The history of Northern Ireland from 1921 to 1972 is a trawling ground for those who wish to lend legitimacy to contemporary political claims. Unionist and nationalist each has his own version, and rarely do the accounts match. Unionists claim that for 50 years Northern Ireland proved itself capable of mature self-government. Nationalists see 50 years of unionist misrule. For each, the era is symbolised by Stormont Castle, which housed the Northern Ireland parliament after 1931: depending on taste, a monument to or mockery of democracy. To unionist, the Stormont years reveal a Catholic minority as disloyal or sullenly abstentionist. To nationalist, Stormont reveals unionism, for all its democratic mouthings, to be a philosophy of favouritism and exclusion, Protestant triumphalism dressed up in social contract theory.

GROWING PAINS

What is the truth of these claims? History usually serves adversarial purposes in Ireland and becomes encrusted with useful myth. Surprisingly, though, it is possible to find places where the different histories meet. Consider the early years of Northern Ireland. Even from the start, each side agreed that the 1920 Act was unsatisfactory. Nationalists (on both sides of the new border) argued that 'Southern' and 'Northern' Ireland would still be under Westminster authority. Unionists (on the northern side) argued that the Act was a stopgap. The provisional nature of the settlement determined early attitudes to 'Northern Ireland'. Unionists were reluctant partitionists but they quickly realised that a divided Ireland over part of which they would be unchallengeable was preferable to a united Ireland in which they would be a minority. They decided to make Northern Ireland work, even if that meant abandoning fellow unionists in the south. Nationalists for their part never imagined that it could work. Northern Ireland, the thinking went, would crumble in the face of renewed fighting or through a redrawing of its boundaries to accommodate nationalist demands.

The Anglo-Irish Treaty of December 1921 brought the war of independence to an end. A peace of exhaustion, it granted fiscal and domestic independence to the 26 county Irish Free State and 'Dominion' status within the British Empire. When Michael Collins signed it on behalf of Dail Eireann he seemed to recognise *de facto* the separate constitutional status of Northern Ireland. But the treaty also made provision for a Boundary Commission to determine how the border might be drawn 'in accordance with the wishes of the inhabitants, so far as may be compatible with economic and geographic conditions'. Here was the nationalists' one hope, the unionists' one fear. A case could certainly have been made for the restoration of parts of counties Tyrone, Fermanagh and Armagh to the Free State, also Derry City. On the other hand, parts of eastern Donegal had a unionist ethos and could have been ceded to 'the North'. In the end, nothing happened. By the time the commission reported, Northern Ireland had been in existence for nearly four years, and the governments of both North and South preferred status quo to any territorial tampering. Their respective minorities would simply have to accept the fact.

From the start the Northern Ireland administration had to defend against IRA activity, some aimed at protecting the Catholic minority from sectarian attack, some aimed at overthrowing the state itself. The state had a bloody baptism. Between June 1920 and June 1922, 428 people died violently and a further 1766 were wounded. The majority of them were Catholic, many the victims of loyalist pogrom, but a substantial number of Protestants also died. The IRA wished to strangle Northern Ireland at birth. Loyalists responded by attacks on Catholics. The government's answer to mounting anarchy was the Special Powers Act 1922 which gave the state extraordinary powers of arrest and detention. It became a source of abiding anger among the minority population. Intended to last a year, the Act remained on the statute book until 1972. By the middle of the 1920s, with the danger of the Boundary Commission past, Northern Ireland had unexpectedly survived beyond infancy, its birth-trauma convincing unionists more than ever that they must take they their stand on partition.

MINORITY WOES

Consider however the position of nationalists. They found themselves a permanent minority in a state whose public rhetoric – Loyalist and Protestant – held no attraction for them. They were abandoned by nationalists in the south. They were considered subversive by unionists, who demanded that they endorse the legitimacy of the new regime. In short, they were left high and dry: disinclined to believe in the permanency of the state but without the means or prospect of altering it. Defeat had been snatched from victory.

Catholics might have improved their lot had they participated in the political life of Northern Ireland in its early years but their cooperation was always unlikely and may not even have been expected. It was unfortunate, too, that when Sir James Craig became Northern Ireland's first Prime Minister he appointed to the most sensitive post in his administration its least sensitive member. This was Dawson Bates, Minister for Home Affairs. Bates considered it his task to maintain the union come what may, even at the cost of electoral sharp practice. He loathed nationalism, and his brief – law and order, local government, the conduct of elections – gave him ample scope to make it obvious. No appointment was more likely to guarantee Catholic alienation from the state.

There was another problem. The political basis of the regime left much to be desired: so also did its financial structure. Most of Northern Ireland's income (roughly 80 per cent) was determined by Westminster. Only minor taxes (such as death duties) could be set in Stormont. From its inception, the Northern Ireland government lacked economic sovereignty. In fact, the need to maintain expenditure on social services at mainland levels meant that the state was often close to insolvency. Keeping up with the English Joneses almost ruined it. The result was further polarisation. Sectarianism became a factor in the division of limited spoils. Hard times brought hard politics, and with the economy itself in decline, it was no surprise that a 'disloyal' minority would bear the brunt.

Northern Ireland thus suffered three weaknesses. Politically, a substantial minority of citizens questioned the legitimacy of the state. Financially, its revenues and expenditures were chiefly determined by others. Economically, its major industries (linen, agriculture and shipbuilding) were unequal to the task of maintaining high levels of employment. There were dire consequences. Scarcity of work pushed people back into their communal redoubts. Protestant tended to employ Protestant, Catholic to employ Catholic: each side 'looked after its own'. Unfortunately there were fewer Catholic employers.

More than anything sectarianism in employment has been deemed the defining characteristic of unionist rule. Catholic unemployment was indeed consistently higher than Protestant, in every cohort, between 1921 and 1972, with many of the differentials persisting down to the present. Additionally, patterns of employment reveal religious cleavage. Catholics formed a disproportionately large percentage of those in lower-paid, semi-skilled and manual work, a disproportionately small percentage of those in skilled manual, lower-grade non manual and professional work. Catholics were under-represented in the police force, the higher civil service, university teaching; over-represented in construction and seasonal trades. But it was unemployment above all which marked the Catholic workforce. The difference between Protestant and Catholic unemployment was and remains substantial. It is a problem exacerbated by its local density in towns like Derry, Strabane and Omagh, and by the fact that Catholic families without a breadwinner tend to be large.

These patterns of unemployment and low-level employment have often been attributed to 'discrimination', official or otherwise, and to an industrial location policy which favoured the predominantly Protestant east of the province over the Catholic west. Yet the notion of 'discrimination' is too crude. It assumes first a deliberate policy to award employment partly or wholly on the basis of religion, and second that all or most Catholic unemployment may be explained in this way. The latter claim, certainly, does not withstand scrutiny. Factors other than denomination were involved: there were twice as many Catholic unskilled manual workers as Protestant, and these had greater chance of being unemployed; Protestants were more likely to be employed in stable public utilities; the large size of Catholic families increased the chances of their being caught in the 'unemployment trap', with little or no marginal benefit to be derived from having a job as opposed to social security. Catholics, in other words, suffered from a combination of disadvantages – structural, educational, locational – which, in a declining economy, severely lowered their job prospects.[1]

Nevertheless, the claim of discrimination has not persisted without reason. Such was the widespread practice in Northern Ireland for many years. Some was low-level: 'looking after your own'. Some was deliberate: nationalists as unreliable, perhaps disloyal. Some was semi-official: 'a Protestant parliament for a Protestant people', as Sir James Craig boasted in 1934. Some was almost self-imposed: a reluctance to apply for posts assumed to be unobtainable. Some was sinister: violence or ostracism at the workplace. It was not hard for nationalists to believe that all of their economic woes were due to this one factor. Many Protestants had no job either, but this was little consolation.

As for industrial location policy, it is both impossible to prove and inherently unlikely that public policy favoured certain areas because they were Protestant. Three considerations may be mentioned in this regard. First, a simple east/west division of Northern Ireland, or even a more specific division, forgets that there were few areas where Catholic and Protestant were not intermingled. Were Protestants west of the River Bann discriminated against in order to get at Catholics? The idea is fanciful and crudely conspiratorial. Second, some of the factors noticed in individual cases of unemployment – namely low levels of skill and attainment – also applied to state-sponsored industrial location. In other words, the quality of the workforce rather than its denomination is far more likely an explanation for industrial location. To some degree, of course, a vicious circle operated. People denied work because they were 'workshy' seemed workshy because they had been denied work. Finally, it should be remembered that government had only a limited role in determining the commercial decisions of companies which might have established themselves in parts of Northern Ireland. There may indeed have been quiet pressure from backbenchers to locate a factory in one area, not another. Whether this amounts to 'discrimination' or to the ordinary exercise of influence as happens the world over is hard to decide.

GERRYMANDER

'Discrimination' is an unwieldy term when applied to employment practices. It can be defined and refined so that grievances may be shown to be false even when they were felt to be real. Discrimination in electoral practice is another matter. There is no doubt that nationalist anger was deepened by the gerrymandering of electoral divisions in local government. Nor is there doubt that the policy was endorsed at the highest levels of the regime. Gerrymandering had the effect of protecting unionist representation in places with a natural nationalist majority. This was not denied. Rather, it was defended on the ground that the state itself would be weakened if parts of it were to fall into 'disloyal' hands.

Derry is a case in point. For years its wards were divided to ensure that a unionist council held sway in a nationalist town, with even the Ministry of Home Affairs (which had jurisdiction in such matters) embarrassed at the extent of the practice. In 1936, for example, when redivision of electoral wards was mooted, an official report found the proposed scheme 'most unsatisfactory', with 'no evidence given in justification' of it. The scheme went ahead none the less (on the grounds that the council was too large) and in the following election of 1938 a unionist majority of 12 to eight councillors was recorded in a town where there were 2000 more nationalist than unionist corporation electors. Lacking power at parliamentary level, it was galling for nationalists to be cheated out of it locally.

HOUSING

More than pride was at stake here. Control of local government had practical consequences, one of the most important being the provision and allocation of publicly-owned rental accommodation for low-income families. Housing was a perennial problem, social and political, in Northern Ireland. Slums and overcrowding seemed a way of life in certain places. Some authorities, however, appeared reluctant to build houses and, once built, to allocate them to Catholic families.

Financial constraint played a part in this, but malign motives were all too readily believed. Not all discrimination was by unionist-controlled councils, and not all unionist councils discriminated. Certainly there is little evidence of systematic anti-Catholic discrimination in housing throughout Northern Ireland. Nonetheless, as the Cameron Commission reported in 1969, favouritism was rife in certain areas – notably Dungannon, Armagh and above all Belfast and Derry – with predictable embittering of community relations.

The Stormont government was forced into action, and in 1971 set up the Northern Ireland Housing Executive (NIHE). By means of the Housing Executive Act (Northern Ireland) 1971, it transferred to the NIHE all housing functions previously performed by more than 60 local councils and development agencies. 150 000 properties were thereby brought under NIHE control. The NIHE's professed aim was to allocate houses to both Protestants and Catholics on a fair and even basis. Despite periodic allegations of fraud and malpractice – the most serious of which were dismissed by the Rowland Commission in the late 1970s – the NIHE has made substantial progress. By 1993, 72 000 homes had been built by it, and the worst aspects of discrimination had been curtailed.

THE POLITICS OF FUTILITY

Jobs, housing, 'discrimination', gerrymander: these were the themes of Northern Ireland's politics for many years. Although distinct, they were all linked in the nationalist mind to the question of partition. Remove the border and the problems of Northern Ireland would disappear with it. This was a naive belief, at times a wilfully escapist one. Unionists took their stand on the border too, ritually ridiculing the achievements of the government south of it, praising those of the government to the north.

It all made for sterile, not to say bizarre, politics. Northern Ireland had an elaborate architecture of democracy – elections, an assembly, a cabinet, a prime minister – but little of the reality. Democracy, narrowly defined as majority rule, was achieved, but at the price of alienation – unionists called it a sulk – of the minority.

The electoral supremacy of unionism was never in doubt, nor indeed that of nationalism in its own pockets of strength. As a result, many seats went uncontested, or only tokenly contested, at election. Cabinet ministers often held their posts for very lengthy periods, sometimes for ten, 15, even 20 years. Nationalists frequently abstained from parliamentary participation: it was not until 1965 that they agreed to form the official opposition. The quality of debate was not high anyway, more a trading of slogans than a mature exchange of ideas. An air of unreality hung over Northern Ireland's democracy. A half-empty chamber met three afternoons a week to consider legislation the passage of which was rarely in doubt. Stormont for much of its life was a place of ghosts.

ENDGAME

This system crumbled at the end of the 1960s, when Northern Ireland emerged from obscurity to dominate world headlines. Why? It may be thought that such a regime could not have long survived. Yet it lasted 50 years and might have lasted longer had not its luck run out.

Several factors hastened the demise: political liberalisation, social transformation, economic expectancy, sectarian fear. Stormont was a reactionary system of government which attempted to reform itself. The result was disaster.

A spirit of change was detectable in the middle 1960s. Northern Ireland still remained a deprived region of the United Kingdom, but since the war it had seen significant improvement in employment, provision of welfare and housing, schools, roads and hospitals. In politics, the old sterilities seemed to fade. Unionism acquired reformist leadership in Captain Terence O'Neill, who assumed the premiership in 1963. Nationalism became less abstentionist. Within the minority, a younger set of leaders emerged to argue that social issues and civil rights, not partition, ought to be the priority. Within the majority, liberal voices could be heard, faintly.

This represented a normalisation of politics. Constant bickering over the legitimacy of the state was evidently leading nowhere. Social, economic, and legal reform offered more fruitful possibilities. Yet sectarianism remained Northern Ireland's besetting sin. Although modest prosperity had been recorded, many Catholics were understandably impatient that its benefits had not been evenly spread. They demanded more, and faster. For their part, working class Protestants under economic threat were reluctant to see new jobs go to Catholics. In the middle was O'Neill, a lugubrious and patrician reformer: too liberal for his party, insufficiently liberal for his opposition, reduced to conciliatory gestures which conciliated no one.

O'Neill's downfall had two immediate causes, from opposing ends of the spectrum: the Northern Ireland Civil Rights Association (NICRA), and the right wing of his own party. Established in 1967, NICRA was a coalition with broad Catholic support and some liberal Protestant elements, demanding abolition of plural voting in local government elections, an end to gerrymandering, fairness in housing allocation, statutory protection against discrimination, repeal of the Special Powers Act, disbanding of the reserve police ('B-Specials'). This was too much for most unionists. Many saw the civil rights movement as subversive and argued (with the circular logic which infuriates reformers) that the demands themselves proved the need to retain the special powers of which the movement complained. Others conceded some merit to the social grievances. But very few saw need to grant NICRA's wishes in full. That would be sentimentalism.

Community relations soured in the later 1960s. The apparent slighting of Derry in the location of Northern Ireland's second university (it went to Coleraine), a meeting between O'Neill and the Irish Prime Minister Lemass (which angered isolationist unionists), and an unfortunate and much-publicised housing case (a Protestant spinster in Dungannon was allocated accommodation over a Catholic family), all contributed to polarisation.

Events tumbled out of control after October 1968. A civil rights march in Derry sparked a riot which was widely reported, alerting British opinion almost for the first time to the problem of discrimination. Yet if the need for reform was now becoming apparent, right wing unionists saw even more clearly the need to resist. Counter-marches led by Reverend Ian Paisley expressed a severe sense of threat.

Paisley, son of a Baptist minister, began preaching at an early age and following ordination established his own Free Presbyterian Church in 1951. Its stock-in-trade was virulent anti-Catholicism. Throughout the 1950s he had been at odds with established Orangeism and Unionism, but by the early 1960s he had acquired a following. In 1963 he led a march objecting to the lowering of the Union Jack at Belfast City Hall to mark the death of Pope John XXIII. He seemed in those days a marginal figure. Still, there was no doubting his potential appeal: a charismatic speaker, by turns passionate and mocking; a 'Big Man' who offered certainties to a community suddenly unsure of itself. He followed in a line of Ulster evangelicals of the nineteenth century – 'Roaring' Hugh Hanna, Henry Cooke – who titillated their flocks with tales of Roman wickedness. The Scarlet Woman has always played well in Northern Ireland.

O'Neill must go, sloganised Paisley, and eventually he did. To accommodate minority demands O'Neill had proposed a five-point reform programme, which included review of local government and suspension of the Londonderry corporation (city council), but not abolition of the business vote, which favoured Protestants. ('One Man, One Vote' was NICRA's most telling slogan.) Facing a split in party and cabinet, O'Neill called a general election in February 1969 seeking approval for reform. The campaign became highly personalised. O'Neill endorsed some candidates, withheld endorsement from others, and the resulting cleavages made his own position precarious. He won only narrow victory in his own constituency (over Paisley), and although re-elected by the parliamentary party his policy was badly damaged. O'Neill resigned in April 1969, claiming that Ulster was 'at the crossroads' between anarchy and reform.

ULSTER AT THE CROSSROADS

Three elements were now apparent: the demand – on the streets – for civil rights; the split within unionism between reformers and resisters; and pressure from Britain to hasten reform. O'Neill's replacement, James Chichester-Clark, found it impossible to reconcile all three. Tentatively reformist at first, he quickly reverted to a law-and-order policy as serious rioting in Belfast and Derry in August 1969 brought the British army to the streets for the first time. The arrival of troops offended unionist pride, signifying Belfast's subservience to London in matters of security, and indicating the failure of the Royal Ulster Constabulary (RUC) to win cross-community support. Unionist sensibilities were further offended by the establishment of 'No Go' areas in Belfast and Derry – barricaded ghettos where the writ of the re-emergent IRA seemed to run.

Why did the dormant IRA awake? It was conspicuously absent in August 1969 when Catholics were being burned out of their homes by loyalists in west Belfast. (This is why the army was greeted heroically in Catholic districts in the early days of the 'troubles'.) By 1970 the army's honeymoon was over. Its role was to police the status quo, not to supervise structural change. As the ghettos turned against the British and the army turned against Catholics the 'Provisional' IRA – a breakaway body from the futile, marxist Official IRA – was able to pose as the nationalists' only protector. By mid 1970, it had roughly 1500 members and a steadily growing supply of guns from the Republic, Britain and the continent.

'Provoism' was a response to the fear of a loyalist 'backlash' against reform of civil rights. In effect, the IRA hijacked the civil rights movement and redirected it towards old-fashioned republican physical force. As for the 'backlash' itself, it took the form of increased support for Paisleyism in Stormont and Westminster elections, which obliged Chichester-Clark to harden his security policy.

Violence sharply worsened in 1971: in the first six months of the year there were 304 explosions, most traceable to the IRA. In March, Chichester-Clark was forced to ask that extra troops be sent, in part to assuage his own right wing. Prime Minister Edward Heath offered 1300 – far too few, unionists argued, to re-take the 'No Go' areas. Indignant, Chichester-Clark resigned, to bring home, he said, 'the realities of the present constitutional, political, and security situation'. Ulster, it seemed, was no longer at the crossroads but had taken the path towards chaos.

Chichester-Clark was succeeded by Brian Faulkner: Northern Ireland's third prime minister in three years, and the last man to hold the office. Faulkner was an instinctive right-winger, unlikely to be trusted by the nationalist community and unable to make more than gestures in its direction. Violence continued to escalate. In August 1971, internment without trial was introduced in the hope of rounding up the 'men of violence'. This was a blunder: it alienated nationalists without greatly assuring unionists. Most internees were republicans, few were loyalists. Moreover, many were IRA men of a previous generation, no longer active, and many real 'men of violence' remained on the streets. Nationalists saw internment as final proof of the illiberality of the regime, unionists worried (rightly) that it would prove insufficient to its task. The IRA congratulated itself on a propaganda coup, one of several at the start of the troubles.

By early 1972 Northern Ireland appeared on the verge of anarchy. Parliamentary democracy (such as it was) had broken down; civil disobedience was rampant; sectarian killing was alarmingly on the rise. A few staging posts should be noticed. On 30 January – 'Bloody Sunday' – 13 civil rights marchers were shot dead by the army in Derr, which led among other protests to the burning of the British embassy in Dublin. On 22 February, seven died in an IRA bombing in Aldershot. On 25 February, a Stormont minister was shot and near-fatally wounded. On 4 March, two died and 130 were injured in a restaurant bombing in Belfast.

It was plain that the Northern Ireland government had lost control of security. Faulkner flew to Downing Street on 22 March to be told by Heath that henceforward law and order should be in the hands of London. Neither Faulkner nor his cabinet was prepared to accept this, and they submitted their resignations the following day. On 24 March 1972 Stormont was suspended, to be replaced by 'direct rule' of Northern Ireland from Westminster. Executive authority was now to be vested in a Secretary of State and three junior ministers, the initial expectation being that this should last for a year. In the event, this arrangement has been extended on an annual basis, often eliciting little parliamentary comment. With one brief interlude (January to May 1974), direct rule has been Northern Ireland's form of government ever since 1972.

NOTE

1 T Wilson, *Ulster: Conflict and Consent* (Blackwell, Oxford, 1988), p.112.

3 DIRECT RULE

The fall of Stormont outraged unionists, gave satisfaction to nationalists, and worried the Heath administration. Political consensus had
disintegrated in Northern Ireland at the same time that sectarian
violence had reached record levels. The new Secretary of State,
William Whitelaw, faced two immediate problems: widespread unionist protest against the end of devolved government, and intensified
activity by the 'Provisional' IRA. The community was more polarised
than it had been since the creation of the state. 'The battle is only
beginning', Paisley had prophesied in 1970. Two years on, it seemed
he was right.

WHITELAW TAKES OVER

Whitelaw's response was secretly to meet leaders of the 'Provisionals'
in July 1972. They demanded that the Irish people as a whole should
decide Ireland's future, withdrawal of troops, amnesty for 'political'
prisoners, an end to internment. The meeting failed. To have granted
concessions would have been to risk the near certainty of loyalist
rebellion. Government sources later suggested that the real purpose
was to give the Provisionals an opportunity to accept peace, expecting rejection. Perhaps: but Whitelaw seems to have expected more
than he got. He had eased internment in his first weeks – 200 were
released – but did not end it entirely. At any rate, when the talks
collapsed he ordered a renewed offensive against 'No Go' areas in
Belfast and Derry, which brought down the physical barricades but
shored up the mental ones.

If anything the political problem was more intractable. The trauma for
unionists of the end of 'their' parliament should not be underesti-
mated: the pain of loss combined with that of humiliation. After 1972
they were disinclined to trust the British government, feeling particular anger that it had been the 'Conservative and Unionist' Party which
had brought them down. Protestant extremism reached ominous
heights. William Craig (O'Neill's Home Affairs Minister in October
1968, sacked in December for his courtship of extreme unionist
elements) formed the Vanguard party. It demanded a return to the

status quo ante or, failing that, 'an independent British Ulster'. Craig promised to make direct rule unworkable. The Ulster Defence Association (UDA), formed in September 1971, was as good as his word. On 27 May 1972 10 000 of its members marched through Belfast in paramilitary garb.

Yet the need for a workable administration was pressing. Unionist fury had hardly cooled when Whitelaw produced a green paper in October 1972 listing options for future forms of government. He urged that an 'Irish dimension' – some kind of formal role for Dublin – should be recognised in any new Northern Ireland government in order to lessen nationalist alienation. A later White Paper, issued in March 1973, made specific proposals:

● Election of a 78-seat Assembly on a system of proportional representation
● Formation of a power-sharing 'Executive' from its members
● Devolution to the Executive of responsibility for social services, industry, education, agriculture, and planning
● Retention of a Secretary of State and junior ministers, but restriction of their concerns to defence, foreign affairs, the judiciary, emergency powers, and electoral arrangements.

The proposals were given the force of law shortly after. The Northern Ireland Assembly Act 1973, passed in May, established the Assembly. The Northern Ireland Constitution Act 1973, passed in July, ended the old political system (of Governor, Parliament, and Privy Council) and granted legislative authority to its successor.

UNIONISTS FALL OUT

Here was an initiative impressive in its ambition and, as it turned out, profound in its consequences. For the first time consensual government was to be institutionalised in the form of 'power-sharing' or, as some preferred it, 'shared responsibility' between Protestants and Catholics. Whether the new structure would reflect or create consensus between the two communities was uncertain.

In one respect, however, it ended a consensus: the initiative destroyed the unionist unanimity of the previous year. Unionists were anxious for a restoration of devolved government, but many were unwilling to accept power-sharing as part of it; nor did they want an Irish dimension. But others were prepared to give the initiative a chance. Brian Faulkner, who had made common cause with Paisley and Craig in the aftermath of Stormont's fall, now began to strike more concilia- tory poses. Paisley and his associates – Craig, Harry West, Ernest Baird – remained adamantly opposed. The rest of the field welcomed the initiative, the nationalist Social Democratic and Labour Party (SDLP) with reservations, the Alliance Party with none.

Table 3.1 Seats won in elections to the Northern Ireland Assembly, June 1973

'Faulkner' Unionists	23
SDLP	19
Loyalist Coalition	18
'Unpledged' Unionists	9
Alliance	8
NI Labour Party	1

Elections to the Assembly in June 1973 (Table 3.1) revealed the extent of the unionist split. The result was excellent for the SDLP, poor for the Alliance party (a middle class cross-community party which stood for consensus and almost nothing else). For unionists the election was a watershed. Whatever way the results were configured, there was a majority in the Assembly for some form of power-sharing, but also a substantial minority strongly resistant to it.

Negotiations ensued between the Secretary of State (who was to broker any agreement) and the various parties. Faulkner played a waiting game, unwilling to commit himself from the start to participa- tion in an Executive but implying that he was available if necessary. The talks came close to collapse on several occasions. To encourage compromise, Heath flew to Belfast on 28 August 1973 and warned of the gravity of failure. In a September interview he implied that if a settlement were not reached there would never be a return to devolved government. Northern Ireland would have to be integrated fully into the United Kingdom. This was the push that Faulkner needed, because the integration option appealed to his anti-power- sharing unionist opponents and thus weakened his own position.

Agreement was finally reached in November 1973 that a three-party Executive be formed of Ulster Unionists, SDLP and Alliance. The following month, the British and Irish governments along with the

Executive parties met at Sunningdale to finalise the 'Irish dimension' of the new arrangements. A two-tier structure was to be established: a Council of Ireland consisting of representatives (30 each) from the Dail and the Assembly, with an advisory role; and a Council of Ministers (seven each, north and south) with limited executive authority over bilateral matters, its decisions to be unanimous otherwise non-binding.

The agreement was only possible because each side had different expectations of it. For the SDLP the Irish dimension was important recognition of the legitimacy of nationalist aspiration. For unionists it was little more than gesture. Faulkner accepted the Council of Ministers with equanimity in the expectation that its unanimous consent requirement would guarantee a unionist veto. Indeed Sunningdale, often condemned as a betrayal of unionism, was a modest victory for it. The Irish government solemnly acknowledged that Northern Ireland's constitutional position could only be changed in accordance with the wishes of the majority of its people. The SDLP made a similar commitment. There may have been less to the Irish dimension than met the eye.

POWER-SHARING

The Executive came into existence on 1 January 1974, with Faulkner as 'Chief Executive' and SDLP leader Gerry Fitt as his deputy. Other ministries were distributed proportionately. This was not a solution to the Northern Ireland problem, but the parties did at least cooperate with maturity and good grace. Faulkner's transformation was notable, from a law and order unionist on the right of his party to a conciliator on the left. The change in the SDLP was impressive too. Here was a party which had been by turns abstentionist or obstructionist in its early years. Given executive responsibility for the first time, it began to recognise that not all decisions of previous administrations had been motivated by sectarian spite.

But difficulties crowded in from the first. Power-sharing was unpopular with the excluded unionists, but the Council of Ireland was anathema. Debates in the Assembly had an ugly quality, accusations of treachery abounding. Faulkner could not enter the chamber without jeers and hisses. Outside, opposition was equally strident. As the Executive struggled to establish its legitimacy it was not helped when the

Supreme Court in Dublin ruled that Sunningdale had not altered the Republic's territorial claim over Northern Ireland. Loyalist fears were thus confirmed by the enemy itself.

In this situation, power-sharing suffered a fatal piece of bad luck: the February 1974 British general election. After two months in office, the Executive had only the fact of its own existence to show that power-sharing could work. There had been no tangible improvement in security, nor much in the way of economic or social progress. The campaign itself was disastrous: the power-sharing parties fought each other for their respective traditional vote and anti-power-sharing unionists formed a united front. The latter won all but one of the 12 seats, and 52 per cent of the vote. The Executive's moral authority collapsed, never to be restored.

Worse was to follow. In protest against the Council of Ireland, a group calling itself the Ulster Workers Council (UWC) – a hybrid body of politicians, paramilitaries and trades unionists – organised a general strike in May 1974. It was an extraordinary episode. Slow to begin, and uncertain of ultimate success, it escalated within two weeks to become a profound challenge to Westminster, Stormont, and the rule of law. Barricades went up in loyalist areas, intimidation was widespread, and – crucially – electricity and power workers came out. The Westminster government was slow to act, the army kept its distance, and the new Prime Minister Harold Wilson gave a famously inept performance on television, describing the strikers as 'spongers'. For loyalists these were heady times.

After 14 days of the strike, unionist members of the Executive resigned, which effectively brought about its demise. It was the second system of government to fail in Northern Ireland in two years. Single party rule had survived 51 years; power-sharing survived five months. The latter experiment was flawed but it deserved better.

THE CONSTITUTIONAL CONVENTION

It was a new Secretary of State, Labour's Merlyn Rees, who witnessed the Executive's fall. Nationalists were especially critical of his weak response to the strike. John Hume of the SDLP complained that there should have been tanks on the streets to quell the disobedience. (Times had changed from the days when *nationalists* had used disobedience to oppose the government of Northern Ireland.) Whatever of this, a grave crisis had been reached. Rees urged a 'breathing space', but he also launched an initiative to fill the political vacuum.

In July 1974 Rees announced that a Constitutional Convention would be established to explore options for government 'likely to command the most widespread acceptance throughout the community'. Nationalists saw desperation here. 'What sovereign government anywhere in the world,' Hume asked, 'would allow part of its territory to decide for itself how it was to be governed, unless it was prepared to let it go?'. The Convention, like the Assembly, was to comprise 78 members elected under a system of proportional representation. Its task, according to Rees's White Paper, was to address three 'realities': power-sharing, the Irish dimension, and the need to obtain Westminster's approval for any proposed scheme of government.

The Convention was intended to be deliberative, but its composition ensured a dialogue of the deaf. Elections were held in May 1975 and results revealed sharp division between anti-power-sharing unionists, the United Ulster Unionist Council (UUUC), and the parties of the former Executive. UUUC candidates polled impressively (46 seats), SDLP (17) and Alliance (eight) did much as before, but the Unionist Party of Northern Ireland (UPNI) – Faulkner's creation, in favour of power-sharing – did poorly, winning only five seats.

Little could have been expected of such a forum. The UUUC demanded 'British parliamentary standards' – a return to majority rule – but was prepared to allow minority parties to chair some parliamentary committees. The other parties sought restoration of cabinet-level power-sharing. There was only one moment when progress might have occurred. Seeking to end deadlock, William Craig – at the instigation of the SDLP – proposed a coalition 'in the national interest' to combat terrorism. For the SDLP this would have provided power-sharing by the back door, but at the risk of alienating their own supporters by associating the party with law-and-order unionism. In fact the idea was unacceptable to law-and-order unionists themselves and was vetoed by the UUUC. Craig resigned the Vanguard leadership and his political fortunes subsequently waned.

The Convention produced a formal report in November 1975 which expressed UUUC thinking: a return to majority rule with some minority parliamentary chairmanships. It was passed by 42 votes to 31. The power-sharing parties produced minority reports of their own. Virtually no movement was detectable on either side, and so it came as no surprise when the Convention was dissolved in March 1976. Rees, perhaps acknowledging that his 'breathing space' should have been longer, suggested that there could be 'no major new initiative for some time to come'.

MASON IN CHARGE

The failure of the Executive in 1974, and of the Convention a year later, suggested two hard truths: that initiatives designed to foster political consensus should not assume its existence in the first place; and that such initiatives could themselves be the cause of polarisation. It was appropriate that Rees presided over both. He seemed to capture the dangers of platitudinous good will, much in the manner of a well meaning schoolmaster who cannot control a class. He was translated to the Home Office in September 1976, and was replaced by Roy Mason, an altogether tougher figure.

With the different personality came a different policy: brisk impatience with initiatives, commitment to making direct rule 'work', renewed emphasis on stronger security, substitution of police and Ulster Defence Regiment (UDR) for army in counter-terrorism. The change reflected Mason's pugnacity, his defence background, and (for all the vigour) a form of political exhaustion – recognition that initiatives had run their course. With Northern Ireland's politicians and its people unable to agree among themselves, the moment seemed right for unsentimental neo-colonial governorship.

Mason had his supporters and detractors. He knitted Northern Ireland more closely to the legislation of Great Britain, which pleased some Official Unionists. On the whole they liked his emphasis on law and order. However, Ian Paisley, leader of the Democratic Unionist Party (DUP), disliked the attempt to make direct rule work, which lessened the chances of a return of a local parliament. In 1977 he and the UDA attempted a reprise of the UWC strike, ostensibly to restore majority rule from Stormont, in reality to claim for the DUP leadership of the unionist camp. Mason faced it down, and within a week the strike had collapsed. As William Craig noted, 'a strike can only bring something down – like the Assembly in 1974 – it cannot build anything up'. From such a source, this was belated wisdom.

Mason's 'Ulsterisation' of security, increased use of undercover agents, and approval of tough interrogation methods, weakened the IRA, forcing it to reorganise itself into small cells. He also reformed the court system. On the other hand, Mason's combativeness was not to every taste. Thoughtful politicians bristled at his indifference to initiatives, and John Hume in particular saw the years from 1976 to 1979 as a wasted opportunity. When his tour of duty was over, Mason claimed that the IRA was weeks from defeat. This was idle boastfulness. Still, if crisis-management was to be the policy, Mason was as good a manager as any.

ROLLING DEVOLUTION

The Executive in 1974, the Convention in 1975: they were flawed experiments because each assumed as given precisely the consensus that each was designed to foster. Here was the Northern Ireland prob- lem captured in miniature: to create consensus within political struc- tures which by nature are designed to reflect divergence. According to nationalists, this instability was both predictable and insoluble. Northern Ireland was (in Charles Haughey's phrase) a 'failed political entity' whose legitimacy had never been accepted by all its people. Unionists disagreed. They cited their desire to remain British as legiti- macy enough for the Northern state. The British line, in public if not in private, was solidly unionist: Northern Ireland would remain part of the United Kingdom so long as a majority of its citizens so chose. But Britain's patience was not infinite and, a return to simple majority rule being impossible, some new structure had to be fashioned.

In the roster of Secretaries of State Humphrey Atkins comes next, but the next significant initiative is that of James Prior. In 1982 he brought some fresh thinking to the problem. Prior proposed that devolved administration should return to Northern Ireland gradually, with more responsibilities being transferred to a local assembly as political con- sensus grew and at a rate that the assembly itself should decide.

This 'rolling devolution' was enshrined in the Northern Ireland Act 1982. A 78-member assembly was to be established, elected in the same manner as the 1973 Assembly. Its role, initially consultative, could be expanded to include executive responsibilities if 70 per cent of its members (fewer if the Secretary of State deemed it appropriate) petitioned Westminster for departmental powers to be devolved to it.

The 70 per cent provision was to ensure cross-party support for any devolution. No single party, in short, should dominate.

The value of the scheme was that Northern Ireland's politicians could themselves set the pace of progress. That was also its vice. Consensus, even about the plan itself, did not exist. Only the Alliance Party whole-heartedly endorsed it. The Democratic and Official Unionists chaffed at a return to power-sharing, the latter vehemently. The SDLP thought it unworkable because it excluded an Irish dimension. Even within the Conservative Party doubts were expressed by 'integrationists' who feared that *any* devolution would endanger the union. Prior countered that his plan would 'tie' Northern Ireland more closely to the United Kingdom – precisely the SDLP's objection to it. The scheme was thus attacked from one side because it tended to weaken the union, from another because it tended to strengthen it. Such are the dangers of ingenuity.

SUCCESS AND FAILURE

'Rolling devolution' suffered the fate of all previous initiatives, and, as with power-sharing and the February 1974 general election, bad luck also played a role. It came at the wrong moment, coinciding with the Falklands War, which stole headlines and worsened Anglo-Irish relations. (Public opinion in the Republic sided with Argentina, with armchair strategists suddenly knowledgeable about the history of the 'Malvinas'.) Elections to the Assembly also dealt it a blow. The SDLP fought on an abstentionist platform – hard to justify in a 'constitutional' nationalist party. Provisional Sinn Fein, also abstentionist, offered candidates for the first time in a Northern Ireland election, winning five seats and an ominous 10 per cent of the vote.

As the Assembly reflected only unionist opinion, a stage-by-stage return to local administration could not be achieved. By its non-participation, the SDLP had effectively exercised a nationalist veto. (Ironically that party has always identified the *unionist* veto as the chief obstacle to political progress in Northern Ireland.) Nonetheless the experiment had some value. For a period, from May 1983 to November 1985, committees of the Assembly scrutinised the workings of Northern Ireland departments on a range of matters from agriculture to education to industrial strategy: the first time that 'direct rule' had been subject to local accountability. Special interests were also able to seek through its committees to influence government policy. This was no bad thing. Policy before then had been generated by unelected civil servants. Moreover, most departments accepted most recommendations. For too long, Prior remarked, Northern Ireland's politicians had enjoyed 'all the advantages of political activity with none of the disadvantages of responsibility'. Now entrusted with responsibility, they had shown some maturity.

The Assembly's character altered radically after November 1985. A new political initiative came to fruition that month, the work of Secretary of State Douglas Hurd. This was the signing at Hillsborough, County Down, of the Anglo-Irish Agreement, which guaranteed the Republic's government some consultative rights in the governance of Northern Ireland. (By the time of the signing Hurd had become Home Secretary, replaced at Stormont by Tom King.) Unionist anger was deep and universal. Thereafter the Assembly became a vehicle for protest – one of dozens up and down the province. It was dissolved on 23 June 1986.

An ill-omened experiment ended ignominiously. It is pointless to speculate on its chances had the SDLP participated and had the Anglo-Irish Agreement not been signed. The ingenuity of rolling devolution and its failure seem to capture something deeper: British rationality confronted with Ulster fierceness, neither comprehensible to the other. When the Assembly closed its doors, unionists and nationalists were farther apart than ever.

4 THE ANGLO-IRISH AGREEMENT

The Anglo-Irish Agreement represents the most significant change in the constitutional status of Northern Ireland since 1920. It was more than another initiative: it established for the first time structures by which the Republic might participate in the governance of Northern Ireland. This was an advance on the grandiose but abortive Council of Ireland of 1974, and a logical development of the British and Irish Intergovernmental Council of 1981. This was agreed at the Thatcher-Fitzgerald summit of November 1981: a rather cumbersome structure of ministers, officials, parliamentarians and advisers intended to provide a forum for Anglo-Irish talks. But it was juridically insignificant. It implied no obligation, Thatcher told the Commons, 'on Her Majesty's Government to consult the Irish Government on matters affecting Northern Ireland'. The 1985 Agreement was altogether more substantial. It accordingly generated a more energetic reaction.

A CONSTITUTIONAL BREAKTHROUGH?

Irish Prime Minister Garret Fitzgerald hailed the Agreement as allowing 'a significant role for the Irish government' within the Northern Ireland administration. He added that it was the Republic's government 'towards which the nationalist minority in Northern Ireland look – just as the Unionist majority look to the Government of the United Kingdom'. The Agreement, he implied, transformed Northern Ireland into a British-Irish condominium. Perhaps he thought that the solution to colonialism was to double the number of colonial powers.

Unionists did indeed look to the government of the United Kingdom – with fury. The Agreement represented betrayal. By contrast, nationalists favoured the new arrangement. At last the legitimacy of their tradition had been given formal recognition by Britain. Some saw it as a staging-post to a united Ireland. Others, however, dismissed it as precisely the opposite: a *de facto*, perhaps even *de jure*, acknowledgement by the Irish government of the permanence of partition. It was thus ironic that both unionists and a small group of the greener elements of the SDLP and Sinn Fein combined to denounce what Gerry Adams called the 'nightmare' of the Anglo-Irish Agreement.

THE AGREEMENT

What were the provisions of the Agreement? Its chief features may be summarised as follows:

Article 1 recognised that the constitutional status of Northern Ireland could be changed only with the consent of the majority of its people and that, at present, no such majority existed.

Articles 2 and 3 instituted the 'Anglo-Irish Conference' of ministers from Dublin and London, to be concerned with Northern Ireland matters, and relations between North and South. Through its structures, the Irish government could make proposals relating to Northern Ireland, but sovereignty remained with the United Kingdom. The Conference was to meet regularly at ministerial or senior civil servant level and was to have a permanent secretariat.

Article 4 pledged cooperation 'for the accommodation of the rights and identities of the two traditions which exist in Northern Ireland' and for the promotion of 'peace, stability, and prosperity'. It also stipulated that the Irish government could make proposals on the 'modalities' of devolution in Northern Ireland 'insofar as they relate to the interests of the minority community'.

Articles 5 to 10 indicated the areas of concern to the Conference. These included:

Article 5 Discrimination, Cultural Heritage, the use of flags and emblems, the possibility of 'some form' of Bill of Rights.

Article 6 Fair Employment, Police Complaints, Human Rights, Equal Opportunity.

Article 7 Security and Prison policy.

Article 8 Legal matters.

Article 9 Cross-border security.

Article 10 Economic and Social development.

Article 11 allowed for review of the Agreement after three years, or earlier if requested.

Article 12 raised the possibility of a future Anglo-Irish parliamentary body along the lines mooted at the November 1981 Thatcher-Fitzgerald summit.

The Agreement was registered at the United Nations on 28 November 1985 and the first meeting of the Conference took place in Belfast on 11 December 1985.

A BREACH IN THE UNION?

As shall be seen in Chapter 9, unionist reaction was unanimously hostile. But was this anger excessive? Here after all was an Agreement in which the Irish government affirmed that any change in the status of Northern Ireland 'would only come about with the consent of a majority of its people'. The Republic also affirmed that the Agreement represented 'no derogation' of the sovereignty of the United Kingdom. These affirmations apparently weakened Articles 2 and 3 of the 1937 Irish Constitution by which the Republic laid claim to the whole island of Ireland as its sovereign territory. In 1937 the Dublin government repudiated the Anglo-Irish treaty of 1921 by drafting a new constitution, subsequently passed by referendum, which remains in place today. Article 2 claims that 'the national territory of Ireland consists of the whole island of Ireland, its islands and the territorial seas'. Article 3 claims for the Dublin parliament and government 'jurisdiction over the whole of that territory'.[1] In 1948 a coalition government under J A Costello (Fine Gael) declared Ireland a Republic, withdrawing it from 'external association' with the Commonwealth. Could it be that unionists, angered by their exclusion from negotiations and offended by the prospect of Dublin's representatives travelling in state to Belfast, had failed to read the small print?

Most serious commentators thought so. There were, however, grounds for unionist concern. How secure was a union in which implicit distinction was made between one part of the United Kingdom and another? Thoughtful commentators noticed that the 'wishes' of the people of Northern Ireland with regard to the union were deemed to be juridically different from those of Scotland or Wales. The result was a weakening of the union into something like creeping federalism. Consider Aughey's analysis:

> The 'present wish of the majority in Northern Ireland is for no change in its British status' [quoting Secretary of State Tom King]... Now this understanding... conveys conditionality; it treats political allegiance as somehow inherently fickle. Tomorrow, next month, in a few years, the majority may 'wish' to be something else. The British government will be only too happy to facilitate that wish, so long as it means Ulster leaving the United Kingdom and becoming part of a United Ireland... Such use of constitutional language by the British government... cheapens the idea of the Union and clearly cheapens the value of its guarantees.[2]

This is fair comment. For a *union* to have meaning, there should be equality between its parts, not some attitude of grateful loyalty to London from Belfast, Cardiff and Edinburgh, or some assumed pre-eminence by London over the rest. The Agreement, Aughey contends, reflects 'the consistent policy of London to be conditional in its loyalty to the United Kingdom'.

If unionists scented betrayal on the part of London, might they have taken comfort, ironically, from the attitude of Dublin? Did the Agreement represent a weakening of the Republic's territorial claim over Northern Ireland? It would seem not. The Irish government was aware of the implications of the Agreement, and took care during and after its negotiation to protect the integrity of the 1937 Constitution. Notice again the language of Article 1 of the Agreement:

> The Two Governments
> (a) affirm that any change in the status of Northern Ireland would only come about with the consent of a majority of the people of Northern Ireland ...

There is more to this than meets the eye. It contains two changes from the Sunningdale agreement which established the Council of Ireland. Sunningdale witnessed separate declarations by each government: this was a joint declaration by both. Moreover, Sunningdale affirmed that constitutional change *could* only come about with the consent of Northern Ireland's majority, whereas the Anglo-Irish Agreement affirmed that it *would* only come about in that manner. The implications are significant:

> The result of the former change was that no declaration at all was made as to what the status of Northern Ireland is, even by the British Government, which at Sunningdale had clearly declared that it was part of the United Kingdom. The result of the latter was that the declaration ceased on one view to have any possible legal as opposed to factual significance.[3]

The importance of the second point became clear when two unionists challenged the constitutionality of the Agreement in the Irish courts. Their case failed, it being held that the Agreement did not violate Articles 2 and 3 of the 1937 Constitution. The judgment of Mr Justice Barrington is worth noting:

It appears to me that in Article 1 of the Agreement the two Governments merely recognise the situation on the ground in Northern Ireland, form a political judgement about the likely course of future events, and state what their policy will be should events evolve in a particular way.[4]

It was thus possible for Irish Foreign Minister Peter Barry to assert that the Agreement was 'totally consistent with the Constitution'.

FIRST REACTIONS

These niceties were politically necessary for the Republic's government, but to unionists they smacked of duplicity. The fierceness of their reaction surprised many. All 15 Unionist MPs resigned their seats, forcing a mini-general election held on 23 January 1986. The tactic worked to the extent that 418 230 votes were cast against the Agreement (44 per cent of the total electorate), but one seat was lost to the SDLP. The Northern Ireland Assembly condemned an Agreement 'designed to operate to the detriment of the majority of the people of Northern Ireland' by establishing 'a joint authority in embryo which ... will become the effective government of Northern Ireland'.

Other reaction was equally predictable. The Alliance party was prepared to give the Agreement a 'fair chance'. Provisional Sinn Fein condemned it as a concession of British sovereignty over Northern Ireland. The SDLP gave it unqualified support (though Belfast City Councillor Pascal O'Hare and some others resigned the party whip in protest against the endorsement of partition which the Agreement apparently enshrined) The party's support was no surprise, since the Agreement gave legitimacy to constitutional nationalism, thus allowing the SDLP to put electoral distance between itself and Provisional Sinn Fein. John Hume's endorsement was fulsome.

THE AGREEMENT IN REVIEW

Unionist fears have not been justified by the operation of the Agreement; nor for that matter have nationalist hopes. Britain has chosen to emphasise that no derogation of sovereignty has taken place. 'At the end of the day,' Thatcher told the House of Commons, 'decisions north of the border shall continue to be made by the

United Kingdom Government.' For its part, the Republic (under different administrations) has shown sensitivity in its use of the Conference, to the extent indeed that some may begin to question its utility.

Has the Agreement worked? Many think not. In February 1988, for instance, 81 per cent of Catholics and 72 per cent of Protestants believed that the Agreement had not benefited nationalists; 94 per cent of Protestants and 88 per cent of Catholics believed that it 'had been of no benefit to unionists.[5] Here was the kind of consensus not planned by the framers. But this perception of failure needs context. Plainly the Agreement has not achieved its first objective – promotion of 'peace, stability and reconciliation'. On the other hand it was not seriously supposed that the Agreement alone could bring about these admirable goals. Yet 'stability and reconciliation' may not be the platitudes they first appear. For nationalists, reconciliation may mean that unionists should reconcile themselves to the permanence of nationalism. So far they have shown no signs of doing so.

And the Agreement's specific purposes? The Inter-Governmental Conference meets amicably two or three times a year, but there has been little change 'on the ground'. Devolution has not been achieved. Efforts have been made to accommodate the nationalist identity, but these have been symbolic, not substantive. More significantly, Britain has taken steps to end job discrimination, establishing the Fair Employment Agency in 1988; but pressure to do so came as much from the United States as from the Conference. On legal matters, the use of 'supergrasses' has ended, but this has been offset by evidence from other quarters of a compromised police force. There has been greater cooperation in border security. Increased economic cooperation has also resulted from the Agreement, but not such as to cause general rejoicing. There is still some way to go if the Agreement is to be considered a practical success.

NOTES

1 *Bunreacht na hEireann* [Constitution of Ireland] (Stationery Office, Dublin).
2 A Aughey, *Under Siege: Ulster Unionism and the Anglo-Irish Agreement* (Hurst and Company, London, 1989), p.25.
3 K Boyle and T Hadden, *The Anglo-Irish Agreement: Commentary, Text and Official Review* (Sweet and Maxwell, London, 1989), p.19.
4 Quoted in ibid.
5 Ibid, p.72.

5 THATCHERISM IN NORTHERN IRELAND

Thatcherism has been the most adverbial political creed of recent times. In the Thatcherite scheme of things, a goal must be pursued resolutely or not at all: the action should speak as loud as the words. This strength of purpose was not to every taste. Where the faithful saw firmness, others noticed inflexibility; where moral conviction, housewifely prejudice. Either way, Thatcher and Thatcherism are hard to separate, and both profoundly influenced politics for over a decade. There were important consequences for Northern Ireland. We have considered already some features of the Thatcher years – rolling devolution, the Anglo-Irish Agreement – but it is well to place them in the wider context of her powerful influence on policy. One of Thatcher's convictions, after all, was that Ulster is 'as British as Finchley'. Examination of both the politics and economics of Thatcherism may modify that conclusion.

THATCHERISM: STYLE AND SUBSTANCE

How then did Thatcherism play itself out in Northern Ireland? We shall consider the economic impact of Thatcherism in a moment. Note first, however, that in a purely political sense, Thatcherism in Ulster was characterised by *infirmity* of purpose. In her first two years in office, Thatcher executed not one but several U-turns, which suggested an analytical incoherence hard to reconcile with 'conviction politics'. Perhaps the incoherence generated the conviction: in the absence of clear thought, after all, stout certainty has its comforts.

The 1979 Conservative manifesto reflected an integrationist approach to Northern Ireland. Making a virtue of necessity, it ruled out an immediate return to Stormont in favour of closer links with Great Britain and modest regional assemblies:

> In the absence of devolved government we seek to establish one or more elected regional councils with a wide range of powers over local services ...

These were the ideas of Airey Neave, who was killed by an IRA bomb shortly before the Tories won power. Neave would have approved of the early direction of policy under Secretary of State Humphrey Atkins. In July 1979 Atkins expressed doubts about the efficacy of devolution. There was too much disagreement between the political parties in Northern Ireland 'even to begin to suggest the possible shape of an acceptable structure of government for the province'.

Yet he had scarcely ruled out an initiative before he embarked on one himself. In November 1979 he proposed that a Constitutional Conference should begin between the parties its aim being a return to devolved government in Northern Ireland. If the prospects for success were slender in July, they were even more so in November. Not only had violence worsened (in separate incidents on 27 August, Lord Mountbatten and 18 soldiers were blown to pieces), but the terms by which the talks were to be conducted made a fruitful outcome improbable. Ruled out of consideration was any discussion of Irish unity, in fact any discussion of an Irish 'dimension' at all. This assured the non-participation of the SDLP. As a result, Atkins was forced to accept an Irish dimension – a concession unacceptable to Ulster Unionists, who boycotted the talks. The Conference ended when the DUP revealed to a disarmed Atkins the extent of its distaste for power-sharing. Such might have been predicted. Such indeed had been predicted – by Atkins himself in July. His attempted amelioration had thus shown the depth of the problem.

No sooner had this effort collapsed – in November 1980 – than a radically different approach was adopted: repairing relations with Dublin as a preliminary step towards an 'external solution'. Thatcher met the Irish Prime Minister Charles Haughey at a summit in Dublin in December 1980. For both parties this was a form of aversion therapy: a substance previously considered noxious was ingested enthusiastically as a cure-all. In Thatcher's case, there was an overdose. Thus the basis of the Atkins talks had been that there would be no Irish dimension. The basis of the summit was that such a dimension might provide a lasting solution. The *communiqué* which followed the meeting spoke of Britain's 'unique relationship with Ireland', and of the need for 'new institutional structures' to express that uniqueness.

This about-turn was naturally upsetting to unionists, the more so as it came from one whom they had cherished as their own. It was now the nationalists' turn to crow. But the turn did not last long. The Irish, mightily pleased with the summit, claimed more for it than was deserved. Foreign Minister Brian Lenihan, popular and ebullient but given to hyperbole, envisioned Irish unity within ten years. This was enough to convince Thatcher that she had been 'bounced' at Dublin, and her attitude once again cooled towards any Irish dimension.

The extent of that coolness became apparent in 1981, when she confronted her most serious Irish crisis to date: hunger strikes of republican prisoners who demanded that they be given 'special category' status. On 1 March, Bobby Sands, leader of Provisional IRA inmates in the H-Blocks, began a fast to dramatise his claim to be a political prisoner. In the course of the next weeks and months, the fast was joined by others. Thatcher refused to yield. Visiting Belfast on 28 May, she declared that the protest 'might well be the last card' that the IRA had to play. Here was Thatcherism in its platonic form: firm, resolute, unyielding. There was nothing ambiguous about a policy which held that to concede special status would be to politicise acts essentially criminal and thereby to legitimise IRA claims to be 'at war' with Britain. As policy, there probably was 'no alternative'.

Nor was there ambiguity about its effects. The strike, and the response to it, made world headlines. Sands, in an April 1981 by-election, was elected MP for Fermanagh-South Tyrone. (The SDLP did not oppose him.) When he died the following month, 70 000 people attended his funeral. A week later, a second hunger-striker died, a week after that, a third. In all, ten died. Each death, each funeral, was accompanied by violence. During the seven-month strike, 64 people were killed in Northern Ireland: 15 RUC, eight British Army, seven UDR, 34 civilians. The Pope sent a personal envoy to plead with Sands. Cardinal O'Fiaich, Archbishop of Armagh, warned that the government would 'face the wrath of the whole Nationalist population' unless it offered concessions. President Reagan was urged by John Hume to intervene. The European Commission on Human Rights and the International Red Cross did intervene.

None of this impressed the Prime Minister. When the strike ended (October 1981), Sinn Fein had received an electoral fillip (in both parts of Ireland), moderate nationalism had been severely embarrassed, and unionism had been greatly cheered. Another policy would have produced, of course, a different configuration of pleasure and dismay: but the hubristic stridency of Thatcher's tone cannot have helped. She had won a costly victory.

To recapitulate briefly. The first two years of Thatcherism in Northern Ireland saw shifting goals and changing priorities. To begin, there was Neave's manifesto commitment to little more than glorified county councils. That was followed by Atkins' devolution initiative (without an Irish dimension) the failure of which was anticipated by Atkins himself. This in turn was modified to include consideration of possible Irish unity. When the modified initiative failed, summitry was attempted. That, too, proved hazardous, and courtship of the nationalist community quickly turned to dismissal. Each policy, in its day, was promoted with the usual rhetorical certainties; but there was little evidence of consistency. During the hunger-strikes even the *Daily Telegraph*, Thatcher's firmest friend in Fleet Street, expressed disenchantment, urging greater 'strength, clarity and purpose in British policy'. This was telling. Be Thatcherite, her supporters seemed to urge.

The advice may not have been altogether sound. Clarity of purpose is no virtue if the purpose itself is flawed. To some, the hunger-strikes showed the danger of forthright leadership in the wrong direction; though on this occasion Thatcher carried British public opinion with her. Preliminary conclusions may nonetheless be drawn. The first is that initiatives in Northern Ireland are fraught with danger. The second is that incoherent initiatives are bound to fail. The third is that personalities do count for something. Atkins and Thatcher thought that they could do business with Paisley: they were wrong. Haughey and Thatcher thought that they could do business with each other: wrong again. These were honest mistakes, but they had consequences for human lives.

A more general suggestion may also be offered: that Thatcherism was more reactive than reactionary. Policy was driven by events more than by preconceived ideology. In fickle Northern Ireland, it can hardly be otherwise. Still, a distinction can be drawn between pragmatism and panic and it was not always well understood in these years.

ROLLING DEVOLUTION OR AN IRISH DIMENSION?

The period which followed did not evince greater coherence. By appealing irony, rigorous pursuit of one orthodoxy – monetarist economics – allowed political experiment elsewhere. When James Prior was exiled as a 'wet' to Northern Ireland he made the province a crucible of initiative. Prior's bluff common sense was attractive, but his policy of rolling devolution was ambitious and unlucky. Moreover, His Mistress's Voice could occasionally be heard in the foreground, booming in different directions.

'Rolling devolution' was ingenious but ultimately futile. It had the appearance of the right answer to the wrong question. Even had its unwieldy apparatus generated consensus, the plan assumed as a sole objective the achievement of inter-party agreement within Northern Ireland. But to the SDLP this 'internal solution' stopped at the point where it should have started. There was no attempt to address the question of the identities of the two communities: what 'Britishness' or 'Irishness' actually meant to each side. The scheme smacked of political science seminar or civil service exam, not of a realistic approach to the problem.

Still, nationalists took hope from Prior's earliest ideas. Before proposing 'rolling devolution', he had hinted at a quite different scheme. In January 1982 he suggested a form of local administration which he believed would be acceptable to both sides because executive and legislative branches would be separate, on the model of the United States. By this scheme, the Chief Executive would be the Secretary of State, who would appoint a cabinet reflecting party strength in the Assembly but also with discretion to appoint non-elected ministers. This latter provision, Prior hoped, would make it difficult for politicians to boycott the Assembly. Thatcher vetoed the proposal.

This was not isolated interventionism. Throughout 1982, Thatcher – seared by the hunger-strike – moved away from accommodation of minority wishes. She opposed the first draft of 'rolling devolution', telling Prior to 'take the green edges off his White Paper'. Insofar as the scheme foundered through its lack of an Irish dimension, the Prime Minister was partly responsible. As for 'rolling devolution' proper, she likely shared the instincts of Tory right wingers, but on this occasion she did not object (as once she had when Prior was Employment Secretary) to a major legislative scheme sponsored by her own administration. One of the more exotic constitutional plans of recent years seems to have got by Thatcher in a fit of absence of mind: much the response of public opinion.

The paradox of Prior's assembly was that, until the Anglo-Irish Agreement, it proved the most harmonious of any since 1974 but the one least likely to work. It was DUP-dominated, and it revealed that, without demons to destroy, Paisleyism could be a surprisingly constructive force. Unopposed, Paisley was as conciliatory as the next man.

To be sure, Thatcher was not fooled by this. In spite of her 'ungreening' in 1981, she knew enough by now of Northern Ireland politics not to repose much trust in a partly mollified unionism. Paisley himself was only half-trained. Her opinion of him, formed at a Downing Street meeting in December 1980, was low. On that occasion he barracked her for the 'treachery' of the Dublin summit, inducing antipathy in response. 'He was a bully, and as a bully herself she took a deep dislike to him.'[1] The evidence of the Assembly notwithstanding, little real mellowing had occurred.

A significant crossroads had therefore been reached by 1984. The Prior initiative was becalmed; Sinn Fein continued to rise; Thatcher had cause to dislike extreme forms of both nationalism and unionism. How would see react, then, to further pressure from Orange or Green? The answer came late in the year. On 3 May, the New Ireland Forum issued its report, analysing the Northern Ireland problem from a largely nationalist perspective and listing three options for future government. The report was a tribute to the skill of Hume, who conceived the idea (to show that constitutional nationalism was not braindead) and who choreographed the contributions of the Republic's three major parties. He also wished to undercut Sinn Fein and to show that 'rolling devolution' had no future. To Prior, however, the report was 'one sided and unacceptable'. To Thatcher it was worse. In November she specifically rebutted its options, declaring all three to be 'out'. This was exquisite embarrassment to Irish Prime Minister Garret Fitzgerald, who imagined he had moderated some of her vigour. It was also a fillip to two unlikely partners: Sinn Fein and the unionist parties.

THATCHER AND THE ANGLO-IRISH AGREEMENT

Yet if 1984 was a crossroads, 1985 was *annus mirabilis*. With the signing of the Anglo-Irish Agreement, Thatcher performed a U-turn more impressive by far than that of 1979-80. Why did she do it? There is no reason to doubt her repeated assertion that she endorsed the Agreement because it strengthened the union:

> I went into this Agreement because I was not prepared to tolerate a situation of continuing violence. I believe in the Union and that it will last as long as the majority so wish...

To the *Economist* this was a hollow boast, indicating ignorance of Northern Ireland's distinctive political lexicon:

> Mrs Thatcher [has] described herself as a 'unionist and a loyalist'. She thus proves that she does not know the sad Ulster meaning of those words. In that province, they imply absolute refusal to collaborate with 'Rome rule', by which they mean the authorities in Dublin; precisely what Mrs Thatcher proposes.[2]

The observation was apt. With entire conviction, Thatcher believed the Agreement to be compatible with the union; with equal conviction, 'unionists' demurred. Either may have been right. Much depended not on the document itself but on its subsequent implementation. The paradox is that in the period after 1985 Thatcher may have strengthened the union by weakening the unionists.

Thatcher's primary justification for action – 'I was not prepared to tolerate a situation of continuing violence' – may be read at different levels. It may mean that she saw the Agreement essentially as a security pact, with some greenish window-dressing to make it acceptable to nationalists; or that it was conceived as a preliminary step towards a long-term solution. The simplest explanation is that it reflected exasperation: at the failure of previous initiatives; at unionist intransigence; at endemic terrorism. According to this reading, it was a treaty of exhaustion, not a deep-laid plot to hand Ulster to her enemies. That would make sense. Conspiracy theories, after all, imply rational calculation, and as we have seen strategic planning seems not to have been a feature of the Thatcher years in Northern Ireland. 'The agreement is patently a long shot', declared the *Economist*: a gambler's optimistic throw.[3]

It was faulty logic to imagine that because previous solutions had failed a radically different one might succeed. Those failures were in part due precisely to their 'Irish dimension'. However, earlier initiatives also failed because of grandiosity and because of British reluctance to see them through. This initiative was different. Not only were its goals modest, but Thatcher, once persuaded, never wavered in her commitment. This was the real significance: that a policy, *any* policy, was maintained over a number of years. The 'clarity and purpose' demanded by the *Daily Telegraph* had been restored to government thinking. Besides, the dangers of another reversal were too high.

It is tempting to offer psychological explanations for Thatcher's determination. Unlike the Atkins talks, the Dublin summit, and the Prior Assembly, this was *her* plan. Also, unionist machismo had to be seen off: Paisley as Galtieri or Scargill, another 'enemy within'. But political calculation also played a part. If this *was* an initiative of last resort, the consequences of not seeing it through would have been dire.

Whatever the reason, an irony should be recorded. It took a policy arguably the most nationalist of any since 1921 to bring out the Thatcherite in Thatcher.

THATCHERITE ECONOMICS: THE PROBLEM

As well as a style of leadership, Thatcherism was a set of economic orthodoxies. The Conservatives came to office in 1979 with four clear purposes: to reduce public expenditure as a percentage of GDP; to control money supply as a way of squeezing inflation out of the economy; to lower the burden of personal taxation in order to encourage enterprise; to reduce borrowing and burdensome debt-service. All were linked. All moreover were seen as answers to long term as well as immediate problems. The aim was to produce a leaner, fitter economy. Corporatism and statism, which had been drags on the economy since 1945 and which had become choking in the 1970s, were to be replaced by smaller government, entrepreneurialism, and personal self-reliance. There was a moral component here, invigorating to Thatcher's friends, infuriating to her foes: a change not merely of government or policy but of culture. Britain was to be Americanised or – as Thatcher preferred – Victorianised: brought up to date by being brought back to the past.

Northern Ireland was ripe for such policies. Its economy was weak and getting weaker in 1979. It faced high unemployment, high levels of state expenditure, a declining industrial base, a non-enterprise culture, low GDP: a microcosm, in particularly dramatic form, of the problems of corporatism. The decline was long-term, though it had been masked for a number of years by a peculiar circumstance. Within Britain, Northern Ireland was an objectively depressed region, but within Ireland as a whole it seemed relatively prosperous.

British levels of social services and state investment nearly bankrupted Stormont. They also meant, and continue to mean, a hefty annual subvention from Westminster simply to keep the economy going. Here is a double irony. Unionists often attributed to their own 'work ethic' a prosperity which was at once chimerical and brought about by someone else's work. Nationalists for their part had grown used to the social services of a state they professed to detest.

There were other peculiar features, most of which have persisted. Considered as one of eleven standard regions of the British Isles, Northern Ireland recorded, and records, extremities in most cohorts: lowest population, lowest population density, highest percentage of population aged 15 or under, lowest percentage over 65, highest birth-rate, lowest death rate, highest percentage of population employed in agriculture, lowest percentage employed in industry, highest percentage unemployed.[4] Even as a regional economy, in other words, it had problems all its own. And this catalogue of imbalances could be continued. Not only had Northern Ireland in 1974 the highest rate of unemployment in the United Kingdom, but by 1988 the rate at which it had risen was higher than for any other place. Rates of long-term unemployment (joblessness for over a year) were also and remain high. On the other hand, house prices are lower than in the rest of the UK. For those in steady, salaried employment, the standard of living in Northern Ireland is high. (So too is the less easily quantified 'quality of life'.) For those without work or skills, the prospects are grim.

The most telling statistic is this: in 1993 45 per cent of all jobs in Northern Ireland are in the public sector, most of them in service industries. The cherished caricature of the left – that the fastest growth industry in 'Thatcher's Britain' was the processing of UB40s – has some plausibility in Ulster. Certainly a great many of its people are state dependents, either for employment or for assistance due to unemployment.

Stagnation is the hazard of such an economy. Multiple services are performed with the state as paymaster – think of teachers, doctors, social workers, prison officers, civil servants, youth training officers, policemen – with little need for enterprise or initiative. Most of the services are necessary, of course, and many fall properly within the domain of the state. Others are essentially make-work. Notice also areas where private sector employment conceals at least some element of state subvention: farmers given subsidies, pharmacists in receipt of dispensing fees, solicitors battening off legal aid, shipyards granted government contracts. Consider, too, Northern Ireland's unique problem: the need to conquer subversion. Terrorism destroys jobs, but combatting it produces them: work (and a great deal of overtime) for policemen, hefty salaries for police and army reservists, to say nothing of 'security' – usually an elderly doorman – for public offices and banks and libraries. Most of this is a direct charge on the national exchequer.

This is to speak only of those in employment. For those out of work, or incapable of it, the state's responsibility is almost total. 'Cradle to grave' provision has spawned an array of presumed entitlements: neo-natal units, child support, school meals, youth training, unemployment benefit, national health, social fund, old-age pensions, the death grant. Thus nourished, a dependency culture can flourish almost without hazard. Nor is this the only drain. To the state as well falls the social cost, easily rendered as an economic cost, of unemployment: all that valium to be prescribed, all that vandalism to be remedied, all that petty criminality to be punished.

Salaries and doles, in other words, form only a fraction of state expense, in Northern Ireland or anywhere else. There is scarcely an area of the economy in which government is not directly involved. It builds and rents houses; it establishes 'enterprise zones'; it trains, retrains, and sometimes employs workers; it builds factories, supplies them with infrastructure, then hopes an investor shall take the bait. 'Rolling back the state' makes bracing rhetoric, but it is difficult to achieve in practice. In Northern Ireland – where the economy is East European in character – the task is even harder.

THATCHERITE ECONOMICS: THE SOLUTION

How then did Northern Ireland fare in the 1980s? It represented a challenge to Thatcherism, with its top heavy public sector, its lack of a secure manufacturing base, its persistently high unemployment, its net receipt of funds from the exchequer. As treatment, cuts in expenditure were indicated, painful as they may have been. Unfortunately monetarism as medicine effects a cure only by making the symptoms worse. Weaning a patient from dependency is not achieved without withdrawal. ('If it's not hurting, it's not working', was John Major's neat summary in 1990.) In Northern Ireland's case, the condition was probably untreatable. Reasons of politics, economics, and simple humanity meant that Thatcherism was never fully applied.

This is not to say that the province was sheltered from national or global trends. On the contrary, the story of the 1980s is that Northern Ireland was hit harder by recession and took longer to recover than the rest of the United Kingdom. The shrinkage of 1979-81 weakened an already sickly manufacturing economy, and this was exacerbated by a Treasury policy of tight money which acted as a disincentive to investment. Part of the difficulty was that Northern Ireland relied too heavily on a small number of heavy employing multinationals – Courtaulds, Michelin, the textile group British Enkalon – and when these scaled back their operations in the early 1980s, the consequences were dire. Nor were outside investors inclined to build factories only to see them blown up. As a result, Northern Ireland did not emerge leaner and fitter in the mid 1980s, merely emaciated.

Unemployment is the best indicator of this. The method of its calculation was altered periodically in the 1980s, but a persistently high level is not to be denied. Throughout the 1980s, Northern Ireland had higher unemployment than any other British region. Moreover, it did not experience the significant falls in unemployment registered in some other regions during the 'Lawson boom' of the late 1980s (Table 5.1).

Table 5.1 Unemployment rates in UK regions, 1981-93

	1981	1983	1985	1987	1989	1991	1993[1]
South West	6.8	8.7	9.3	8.1	4.5	7.1	10.0
South East	5.5	7.5	8.1	7.2	3.9	7.0	10.5
West Midlands	10.0	12.9	12.8	11.4	6.6	8.6	11.5
East Midlands	7.4	9.5	9.8	9.0	5.4	7.2	9.7
East Anglia	6.3	8.0	8.1	7.3	3.6	5.8	8.6
North West	10.2	13.3	13.7	12.5	8.5	9.4	10.9
Yorks/Humberside	8.8	11.4	12.0	11.3	7.4	8.7	10.6
North	11.7	14.6	15.4	14.1	9.9	10.4	12.1
Wales	10.4	12.9	13.6	12.0	7.3	8.7	10.3
Scotland	9.9	12.3	12.9	13.0	9.3	8.7	9.9
Northern Ireland	**12.7**	**15.5**	**15.9**	**17.0**	**14.6**	**13.8**	**14.7**

1 Figure for 1993 is January only
Source Department of Employment

The high birth rate played a part. In essence, the work force expanded as manufacturing contracted. (In addition, more women than before entered the labour market, with the consequence that the percentage figure for female *unemployment* increased.) Overall, the effect was that Northern Ireland shifted even further from manufacturing towards a service economy. Between 1979 and 1989, 40 000 manufacturing jobs were lost, most in the early 1980s but at least 5000 of them from the middle of the decade, when the rest of the UK experienced growth. Public sector and service employment could only take up so much of this slack. And the higher female percentage of the workforce had a depressing effect on average wages, as many entered low-skill occupations. By the end of the decade the economy was more reliant than ever on state subsidy and less productive to boot.

In no meaningful sense can 'Thatcherism' be said to have been the cause of these changes. It may have acted as catalyst for some of them, but even this needs qualification. If anything, Northern Ireland was relatively protected from supply-side economics. Ian Aitken of the *Guardian* described it in 1989 as an 'independent Keynesian Republic ... where monetarism remains unknown'. Journalistic license apart, this contains the core of the matter. Thatcherism did not fail in Northern Ireland: it was scarcely attempted. The view of some commentators – that these years saw 'slavish commitment to the touchstone of monetarism'[5] – is hard to sustain.

THE 'KEYNESIAN REPUBLIC'

Consider the stewardship of James Prior. During his time in office an old-fashioned economic *dirigisme* prevailed. 'In Northern Ireland we're all Keynesians,' he remarked in 1983. Prior created a new Department of Economic Development out of the old Commerce and Manpower departments. He established an Industrial Development Board (IDB), with the brief of attracting inward investment through grants, subsidies, interest-free loans, and advance factories. Another body, the Local Enterprise Development Unit (LEDU), also flourished, its task the promotion of small business. Prior had no open cheque-book – retrenchment remained Treasury policy – but Northern Ireland did reasonably well. In 1983 he announced significant measures to attract investors: a refund of corporation tax to a maximum of 80 per cent, a 100 per cent de-rating of industrial premises. Other places might have been so lucky.

The political component of industrial strategy should not be over-looked. It took two forms. First, successive administrations have assumed that the devil makes work for idle hands. Second, they have also assumed that there would be the devil to pay if hands once busy become idle. Whereas on the mainland the social cost of unemployment or redundancy was often accepted, in Northern Ireland there would have been a political price as well, especially if those made redundant were loyalists. If Provoism could be said to be the price for decades of underinvestment in nationalist areas, there was no desire to repeat the mistake among working-class unionists. Ministers certainly saw public funding as a salve for Northern Ireland's political sores. Economy minister Richard Needham expressed a conventional wisdom in 1989:

> If work can be found for the ... 10 000 unemployed boys in West Belfast, that in itself will do more to impact on the political and security areas than anything else.[6]

Such had also been the thinking of the previous Labour administration. Unfortunately the De Lorean Motor Company was poor advertisement for it. Intended as West Belfast's salvation, it failed in 1982 with debts of over £100 million. Loss of public money was equalled only by loss of government face.

Finding employment for Catholics of west Belfast may have been expensive, but nowhere near as expensive as maintaining employment for Protestants to the east. Throughout the 1980s, Harland and Wolff and Short Brothers (ship-builders and aircraft manufacturers respectively) were Northern Ireland's two largest single employers, their workforces overwhelmingly and vocally loyalist. Both companies had received massive public subsidy over the years, rendering them virtually state-owned. Yet each faced trouble in the Eighties. The ship-yard – largest in the UK – could not buck long-term shrinkage of its market. A workforce of 40 000 at the end of World War Two had contracted to less than 4000 by 1985. Closure could have been justified on economic grounds: an EC report argued as much. Instead, state subsidies to the yard amounted to £68 million in 1986. 'Short's' was less of a dinosaur – there is still a demand for its product – but despite good contracts (£125 million from the RAF in 1985, £225 million from the Ministry of Defence the next year) it still reported losses of £35 million in 1986.

Together the companies provided nearly 10 per cent of all manufacturing jobs in Northern Ireland, and received about a third of all state funds for industrial support. Neither could have survived a dose of pure Thatcherism. On the other hand, neither could expect immunity. A decision was therefore taken to 'privatise' both. Politicians of all stripes protested. But free-market principles work both ways. For an enterprise to be sold there must first be a buyer, and perhaps some preliminary fattening to that end. In the case of Harland and Wolff, a management-worker buy-out was contemplated, nicely in keeping with Thatcherite thought. Yet this too would cost money. Around £500 million was contributed from the public purse to enable the buy-out to take place. As for Short's, a Canadian firm, Bombardier, took it off government hands in 1989, but not before some £760 million had been allocated to make the sale possible.

Economists can decide whether this represented an abandonment of *laissez-faire* or an embrace of it. Either way, zeal for free markets came face to face with the market itself, and the result was a more pragmatic approach to privatisation than in other parts of the UK. This may be noticed in other areas of industrial strategy. Consider small and medium-sized businesses. These were and remain vital to an economy such as Northern Ireland's, and promotion of them accorded well with Tory policy. But did the government get a good return on its investment? Probably not. Jobs created through public funding are invariably more costly than those generated purely in the private sector, and while this expense can be justified if the result is an economy eventually capable of looking after itself, such was plainly not the case in Northern Ireland. The Northern Ireland Economic Research Centre reported in 1989 that there was little to show for the policy of successive governments of state support for small and medium-sized companies:

> After three decades of intensive policy assistance and the expenditure of several billions of pounds at 1988 prices, only 109 assisted firms remained in 1986 employing 21 742 people (approximately one fifth of total manufacturing employment).

These were good jobs, to be sure, but created at a very heavy price. A market purist might have been inclined to cut his losses. Not so the government. It spent £208 million in such subsidies in 1986, and although there were the usual complaints about value for money, it showed no sign of entirely abandoning the policy.

There was no likelihood of this when even ministers who were on the right of the party seemed to go native once appointed to Northern Ireland. Wets did not go there to dry out: it was the other way round. The inveterate instinct of politicians – to boast of actions which cannot be avoided – came to the fore. By the end of the decade, ministers routinely made a virtue of public spending necessity. The figures were on their side. As Gaffikin and Morrissey report,

> In 1980-1, public expenditure per head in Northern Ireland was about 33 per cent greater than in Britain. By 1986 this had increased to 42 per cent... [In 1990] public expenditure per head for the four countries of the UK was as follows: Northern Ireland, £3626; Scotland, £2805; Wales, £2489; England, £2161. The average for the UK was £2275.

Thus continued an historic pattern. Because Northern Ireland has always contributed less in taxes than it receives in revenues, the Treasury has always been obliged to make up the shortfall. In fiscal year 1988 to 89 this 'British subvention' amounted to £1.6 billion, £1.9 billion including the cost of security. In fiscal year 1992 to 93 it had risen to over £3 billion.

SOCIAL COSTS

A perception has nevertheless persisted that Northern Ireland suffered because of 'Thatcherism'. Throughout the decade, politicians, academics, the social welfare industry, all combined to deplore its ravages. 'The cuts' became a mantra, endlessly repeated, hypnotically consoling: one of the few political unifiers in a divided land.

It would be wrong to imagine that Northern Ireland's politicians suffered from collective delusion, condemning as parsimony what they ought to have hailed as largesse. Some of their criticism of Thatcherism was foolish – as of a patient blaming the illness on the diagnostician – and some of it merely metaphorical – the term an all-purpose moan about Ulster's economic ills. But some was justified.

Consider regional comparisons. That Northern Ireland was 'doing better' than other places does not necessarily mean that it was doing well. Such a comparison, moreover, may also say something about the other places. The province in some respects certainly did well, but if ingratitude was the general response, that is because disappointed expectations rarely take comfort from the greater disappointment of others. Northern Ireland may have been shielded to some degree from general retrenchment, but it did not escape.

Consider also allocation of funds. Even excluding expenditure on security, much of the 'extra' spending in Northern Ireland was devoted to the satisfaction of social needs long since satisfied on the mainland. Much catching up had to be done in the matter of hospitals, neo-natal provision, and the like. Thus politicians could justify 'special treatment' simply on grounds of parity, not special privilege. When these adjustments are made, the per capita margin of public expenditure in Northern Ireland over other regions shrinks almost to zero.

THE PROBLEM OF POVERTY

For all that, the impact of Thatcherism in Northern Ireland should not be judged as a matter merely of regional relativity. Individual lives were affected by it. Social security is the best case in point. Northern Ireland, along with the rest of the United Kingdom, saw major changes in funding and distribution of benefits for those without work or otherwise in low-income categories. The changes were enshrined in the Social Security Act 1986 which came into force in April 1988. Its purpose was to simplify and rationalise a system which had become hard to understand and hard to defend; to 'target' specific need; to loosen the rigidities of the labour market by making employment differentially more attractive than state-supported idleness; to ameliorate real hardship. The Act's main provisions were abolition of supplementary benefits, to be replaced by income support; abolition of family income supplement, to be replaced by family credit; abolition of special payment grants, to be replaced by discretionary loans from a 'social fund'; and changes in housing benefits. A later measure – the Social Security Act 1989 – imposed tougher 'availability for work' criteria, to make it harder for a claimant to decline employment, 'suitable' or otherwise, should it come his way. The package as a whole shifted the emphasis in social security from grants to loans, in keeping with a view of 'entitlement' as entrapment in low income, demoralising for the individual and expensive for the state.

Government supporters hailed this as an assault on poverty; critics charged that it was an assault on the poor. It was grounded, certainly, on an old distinction – between the 'deserving' and the 'undeserving' poor, the latter like 'sturdy beggars' of Elizabethan times, able to work but unwilling. The dichotomy is a doubtful one, socially stigmatising and to an extent self-perpetuating. The existence of the workshy may be taken for granted in most societies. But policies based on the presumed empirical reality of the two categories are likely to be flawed.[7]

Northern Ireland, with its high level of state clientage, was much affected by the changes; adversely so, in the view of a sizeable lobby. That some regression was apparent is unsurprising: such is inevitable if employment is to be made more attractive than unemployment. But the extent of the regression may have surprised even the government. 'Targeting' turned out to be cock-eyed, sometimes missing the object entirely. Those most in need of loans from the social fund, for example, were often those with the highest levels of debt. This was likely ground for refusal, debt being a sure sign of 'undeservingness'. By contrast, those entitled to loans often refused them: a case of the 'deserving' poor making themselves poorer. There was a kind of perversity in both instances. If so, the policy may be faulted for philosophical confusion. Its attempt to eliminate real hardship jarred with another unspoken requirement: that an underclass of sorts should exist as an incentive for most people not to fall into it.

Northern Ireland had its dose of medicine after all. Some undoubtedly lost out. Local charities reported a strong demand for their services, often from 'first time' users: a case (some held) of 'privatising the poor'. Some social fund officers admitted a presumption against making discretionary loans, so that (unlike the previous system) treatment of objectively similar need varied from place to place. Ministers themselves acknowledged that allocations to the social fund were lower than previous allocations to supplementary benefits, and that in the system's first year of operation every social security office in Northern Ireland *underspent* its allocation. (With circularity, critics of the poverty lobby claimed this as proof that they had been right all along.)

Did it work? Before the measures came into force, and for some time thereafter, Northern Ireland experienced a fall in unemployment. Very little of this was caused by real growth in the local economy: most of it was due to the jobless finding work in Great Britain, where expansion had boosted demand for labour. Simple chronology makes it impossible to attribute all or even most of this mobility to the reforms; nor can it be said that mobility would not otherwise have occurred. There were, besides, factors making for immobility – more so in Northern Ireland than in other parts of the country. Still, a case could be made that at least *some* of the willingness to seek employment elsewhere was a result of the changes. All sorts of reasons made certain groups reluctant to 'take the boat': but some did. In more ways than one it was a bitter-sweet experience, for not only was there the pain of leaving home, but also the recognition that it was in 'Thatcher's Britain' after all where the work was to be had.

UNEMPLOYMENT: THE ABIDING AILMENT

For all that, joblessness shall be the memory of the economic management of Northern Ireland in the 1980s. But care is required in assessing causes. To see 'Thatcherism' as the demon is unsophisticated: that leaves out a multiplicity of other factors, not least continuing terrorism. It also posits a greater stringency in public expenditure than was actually the case. Most of all, it assumes that things might have been different under different management. Would that have been the case? We cannot be sure, but it is unlikely. A 1991 survey of Northern Ireland's economic prospects saw future gloom, no matter which party held power:

> There seems little likelihood that the unappealing prospect of unemployment continuing at close to 15 per cent can be avoided through job creation. Even the advent of a Labour Government less opposed to increases in public expenditure could do little to increase growth in Northern Ireland in the short term, given the probable national constraints on public finance...[8]

Good times, it seems, are not around the corner just yet.

NOTES

1. E Moloney and A Pollak, *Paisley* (Poolbeg Press, Dublin, 1986), p.380.
2 *Economist*, 23 November 1985, p.49.
3 Ibid.
4 Central Statistical Office, *Regional Trends 28* (HMSO, London, 1993).
5 C O'Leary, S Elliott and R A Wilford, *The Northern Ireland Assembly 1982-1986: A Constitutional Experiment* (Hurst and Company, London, 1988), p.115.
6 F Gaffikin and M Morrissey, *Northern Ireland: The Thatcher Years* (Zed Books, London, 1990), p.90.
7 L Howe, *Being Unemployed in Northern Ireland: An Ethnographic Study* (Cambridge University Press, Cambridge, 1990), p.3.
8 Northern Ireland Economic Research Centre, *Economic Forecasts for Northern Ireland* (March 1991), p.7.

6 UNIONISM AND NATIONALISM

The 'troubles' have made fatalists of the people of Northern Ireland. 'Nothing ever changes,' they say. But this is far from the case. The two main traditions, unionist and nationalist, and the parties which enshrine them, have had to modify their identities over the years. In part this reflects a need to respond to the 'other side'; in part a need to protect from rival positions within one's own tradition. This chapter attempts to trace the adjustments made necessary by a generation of civil disturbance and political flux.

UNIONISM

For years unionism was the most easily expressed of Northern Ireland's political creeds yet the most inarticulate. The union meant the link with the Crown, it meant Stormont, it meant the 'British way of life': simple certainties. Deeper questions went unanswered because they went unasked. Was the union *for* something or was it an end in itself? What was the proper institutional relationship between Great Britain and Northern Ireland? Did the 'will of the majority' constitute sufficient legitimacy? A majority of what – six counties, four counties, three? Unionism had little to say about these matters. 'A Protestant parliament for a Protestant people' and 'What we have we hold' sufficed for political philosophy.

The loss of Stormont changed everything. It forced unionists into articulacy, indeed self-awareness. Subsequent events – power-sharing and the Anglo-Irish Agreement – also induced fundamental re-examination of the relationship with the rest of the United Kingdom. Paradoxically, the fiercest unionist language of recent years has been directed towards London, not Dublin, on the grounds that the latter is at least predictable, whereas the former is treacherous. Nationalists point to what they see as the logic of this: that a 'unionism' which repudiates the United Kingdom's parliament and government is no unionism at all. Unionists have an answer of sorts – that their loyalty is to the state itself – but reaching it has not been easy.

The reinvention of unionism has taken place at a time of lost hegemony. Power had been for so long the natural order of things for unionists that, deprived of it, their self-confidence vanished, to be replaced by bellicosity and rhetorical extravagance. As a result, their demands for restoration of 'local democracy' have seemed so much special pleading, a form of the old bigotry. Nor have they helped their case by the apparent sourness and narrowness of their imperatives. Rejecting power-sharing and closer links with the Republic, unionists risk themselves being rejected by British public opinion.

Lost hegemony has been paralleled by lost harmony. Even before the beginning of direct rule in 1972, the unionist monolith had been in danger; after, it collapsed. For years, the Ulster Unionist Party had a monopoly of power. It was an impressive coalition of landed gentry, industrialists, and Protestant urban and rural working class, usually commanding 40 or so of Stormont's 52 seats. Social deference, shared Protestantism, economic self-interest, and sentimental Britishness held it together. As we noted, the reforms of the 1960s caused strains. The Democratic Unionist Party, launched by Ian Paisley in 1971, emerged to appeal to working-class Protestants who feared civil rights. Its first chairman, Desmond Boal, promised a party 'right wing in the sense of being strong on the Constitution, but to the left on social policies'.[1] This was a clever combination, as the party was never required to implement its social populism. In the mid-1970s, unionism disintegrated into bewildering rivalries. Since then, the chief division has been between the Ulster (or 'Official') Unionist Party (OUP) and the DUP. The former is much reduced from its heyday, but remains the largest single political grouping in Northern Ireland.

THE OFFICIAL UNIONIST PARTY

Official Unionists come in two varieties: devolutionists and integrationists. Devolutionists dominated the party for most of the 1970s. Having lost Stormont, they simply wanted it back. Compounded of nostalgia and self-pity, the policy played well for a time in village halls, but not at Westminster. When it dawned that the status quo *ante* was unattainable, new approaches were tried: majority rule with small concessions to the minority; majority rule with a bill of rights; regional councils as a step towards a new majoritarian assembly. All assumed that the best form of government for Northern Ireland was one directly elected by the people of Northern Ireland. The assemblies of 1974, 1975, and 1982 cast some doubt on that proposition. There is more to the devolutionist wing of the party than nostalgia; but not much more. Consider the Charter Group. Formed in 1986 in response to the Anglo-Irish Agreement, it offered a 'New Charter' for Northern Ireland: return to 'a full-blooded devolved legislature at Stormont'. The new charter was old hat. Prelapsarian innocence may be noticed in its twin beliefs that an unreconstructed Stormont was desirable and that the 'irrevocable cultural political identity' of Northern Ireland made it necessary. The group commanded little support.

An 'integrationist' wing thus emerged in the party, for four reasons: as a recognition of the unlikelihood of devolution; as an application of the logic of direct rule; as a conviction that devolution had been an aberration in the first place, unwanted by true unionists in 1920; and as a belief that equal UK citizenship would remove Northern Ireland's politics from the crucible of sectarianism. The debate between devolutionists and integrationists provides the major dynamic of OUP politics today, with the latter on top.

So, Stormont – once an article of faith – is now dispensable. Why? In the first instance, devolution itself is increasingly viewed as an historical aberration. A Belfast parliament was accepted in 1920 only as a means of remaining within the union: it was never the essence of unionism. Moreover, it proved an ambiguous bulwark. Designed to bind Northern Ireland to Britain, it had the effect of permitting it (with dire results) to develop differently. Successive British administrations regarded Northern Ireland as a place apart precisely because, unlike Scotland or Wales, it had its own parliament.

These arguments were made as early as 1971 by Enoch Powell, to whom integrationism owes its intellectual pedigree. Powell claimed that Stormont itself was the chief threat to the union, because it was 'an assertion of separateness'.[2] Few agreed with him, but his election as Ulster Unionist MP in 1974, and that of Molyneaux as party leader in 1979, strengthened the integrationist wing. Molyneaux, under Powell's tutelage, has consistently argued the case for an ever closer union, in which it appears the nationalist problem shall be solved simply by being ignored.

INTEGRATION

What *is* integration? It differs from direct rule in that it opposes special treatment for Northern Ireland within the United Kingdom. Equal citizenship is its core demand: an attractive proposition because it seems to offer the possibility of non-sectarian unionism. In practice it would require that Northern Ireland be legislated for at Westminster in the same manner as England, Scotland and Wales, not (as is presently the case) by means of Orders in Council. It would also mean reform of local government, again to bring Northern Ireland into conformity with mainland practice. Finally, and crucially, it would require that British political parties organise themselves in Northern Ireland.

This last has proved the sticking-point, and not simply because the parties have shown no enthusiasm for it. Without it integration makes no sense, for only thus would the people of Northern Ireland be able to vote for their government. Some integrationists prefer to make administrative integration the priority, leaving political integration to come at some later date. Others advocate the latter. The division has embarrassed the party leadership, which is reluctant to embrace the self-dissolution its own policy logically implies. The strongest supporters of political integration have been marginalised within the party, some expelled. Not coincidentally, they have also been the most consistent advocates of a liberal, pluralist unionism.

THE DEMOCRATIC UNIONIST PARTY

Throughout the 1970s the DUP made impressive progress, steadily eroding the OUP's electoral hegemony. The party's high water mark came in 1979 when Paisley polled 29.8 per cent of the total vote in elections to the European parliament. (Uniquely in the United Kingdom, Northern Ireland is a single constituency returning three MEPs by proportional representation.) Since then it has fallen back, but a changed geography is still apparent. The DUP combines appeal to working class Protestantism and rural evangelicalism, a substantial bloc. It tends to do better in times of crisis, a tribute to Paisley's uncompromising politics. In recent years, however, the 'Big Man' has seemed trapped by his own bluster. The Anglo-Irish Agreement may prove to have been one crisis too many. The Agreement was a double blow. It embarrassed his efforts to build a base using the 'rolling devolution' Assembly of 1982-86. Moreover, unionist unanimity against the Agreement blurred the distinction between DUP and OUP, to the point where it seemed as if the two parties simply acted as one.

The DUP remains committed to devolution, not integration. A return to the status quo ante 1972 seems to be the goal. 'I want as much power as possible' for any Assembly, Paisley urges, with decisions made on majority vote. The wishes of the minority? These would be accommodated not by power-sharing but by some unspecified arrangement with the government of the Irish Republic. The arrangement would be modest in scope, limited to matters of mutual interest – agriculture, cross-border cooperation, industrial development. It is hard to see how this would satisfy nationalist aspirations. An irony, however, may be recorded. The DUP's agenda for the 1990s – Stormont majority rule, minority conciliation by gestures towards the Republic – seems remarkably like O'Neill's agenda of the 1960s, opposition to which gave Paisley his political start.

How democratic is the Democratic Unionist Party? Indeed, how unionist is it? It remains very much its leader's creation, and shares his personality – brash, fundamentalist, anti-intellectual, and defensive. If (as a rule of thumb, no more) Official Unionists are Church of Ireland, Democratic Unionists are Presbyterian – with a longer memory of the fate of their ancestors from Scotland in 1641. This lends crusading certainty to Paisley's position as party leader. As for the party's unionism, that may be challenged on two grounds. The insistence on devolution begs the integrationist questions which we noticed in the section above. Likewise the union itself may be for the DUP only an instrumental loyalty, primary allegiance being to an independent Protestant Ulster.

Some suggest that the party is not only undemocratic but positively fascistic. That the claim could be made is significant, even if it seems strained. Its working-class appeal, its fondness for marches, flags and street protest, and its extreme demonology, all hint at a sinister side. Those who deny the charge do not always sound convincing.[3]

NATIONALISM

The nationalist identity has become altogether more complex since the days when removal of the border was its only demand. For years, anti-partitionists relied on simple ethno-geographical determinism:

the people of Ireland were one, the island of Ireland was one, therefore the governance of Ireland should be one. This enabled them to notice the absurdities of enforced political division: a border which ran through fields, roads and rivers, a unionist party which refused to admit that the rest of Ireland existed. It also required nationalists to believe that unionist desire to be British was evidence of false consciousness – the result of irrationally fearful Protestantism or wilful misunderstanding of 'Irish' culture, or absurd anglophilia. Finally, it helped them explain the relative failure of social politics in Northern Ireland for over 50 years.

These simplicities no longer suffice. Nationalists, like unionists, have been forced into self-redefinition in recent years. The distinctiveness of the unionist culture has had to be acknowledged, not least because of its resilience in the face of violence. There has been recognition that unionists cannot be forced – and certainly not persuaded – into the Irish Republic as it is presently constituted. A more pluralist nationalism has resulted. There is greater willingness now to talk of the 'peoples' of Ireland, of separate traditions requiring mutual acceptance. This may be the old ethno-geographic determinism dressed in liberal language, but it is as far as nationalists can go by way of accommodation and still remain nationalist.

THE SOCIAL DEMOCRATIC AND LABOUR PARTY

The SDLP has been the chief vehicle for constitutional nationalism in Northern Ireland since its foundation in 1970. Its electoral appeal is broad. Both middle-class and working-class Catholics are comfortable voting for it, though not all of them do so, some of the former choosing Alliance, some of the latter Sinn Fein. Left of centre social policies and Irish unity by consent have always constituted its agenda. The one variable has been its attitude to Northern Ireland itself. Participation in government in 1974 implied an endorsement of the institutions of the state, an embarrassment for a nationalist party only slightly eased by insistence on the Council of Ireland. Since then the party has had to balance the claims of an internal solution (essentially, power-sharing) and an external one (emphasis on the 'Irish dimension' to the point of reunification). Under the influence of John Hume, party leader since 1979, the SDLP has steadily favoured the latter course, without abandoning the former.

What, then, is the SDLP analysis? According to Hume – easily the most substantial thinker of the main parties – three sets of relationships have to be addressed before any solution can be proclaimed:

> There is one in the North [between the two communities], there's the one between Unionists and the rest of the island and there's the British-Irish. But the central relationship, the most fundamental one, and the one that goes to the heart of the problem is the Unionist relationship – or lack of it – with the rest of the island, or in more clear terms, the Unionist distrust of the rest of the island ... Until that relationship is resolved, nothing will be stable or lasting.[4]

There is paradox here. Unionists deny Hume's premise, but in so doing they validate his conclusion. To them, the relationship with the rest of the island is *not* central – witness their insistence that the problems of Northern Ireland should be solved by the people of Northern Ireland – precisely because they do not trust the Republic. This is the logic of perpetual frustration: every gesture of conciliation is viewed as yet more subtle entrapment. The greatest trap to date, unionists believe, has been the Anglo-Irish Agreement.

Adherence to the Agreement is central to SDLP policy in the immediate term. For the first time, the party argues, Britain has formally acknowledged neutrality on the question of Irish unity. If the wish of the people of Northern Ireland is for unity, according to Article 1(c) of the Agreement, then Britain would introduce legislation to that effect. Unionists can therefore no longer rely on having their unionism automatically underwritten by the British government. They retain, of course, a natural veto on any new form of governance for Ireland – their wishes remain as valid as before – but not the 'unnatural' veto of British support for any position they care to adopt.

This being so, it makes sense for unionists to engage in dialogue with the Republic. That indeed should be their priority, more than talks with the SDLP, because the latter dialogue would assume an internal solution which the SDLP itself considers unattainable. In essence the argument is that unionists have been abandoned by Britain and they should recognise the fact sooner rather than later. Deputy leader Seamus Mallon has expressed the point with characteristic economy: 'their real future lies in this island, in their relationship to us and their relationship with the Republic of Ireland, and not with a British government which treats them as "paddies" as they treat all of us'.[5]

Alone, this line of reasoning is evidently flawed. Unionists have not inferred from their abandonment by Britain – if such has been the case – that their best hope lies now with the rest of the island. Independence remains an option. The second line of SDLP attack therefore has been to point to the futility of that course – it would lead to economic weakness and political instability – in order to reinforce the inevitability of an all-Ireland settlement. In reality, however, the very ineluctability of this logic has had the opposite effect. 'Dialogue' is now considered by unionists to be SDLP code for *fait accompli* unification: evidence of the wide gulf between them.

What is the nature of the all-Ireland settlement which the party deems to be inevitable? By definition it is negotiable. Hume's preferred solution, as far back as the New Ireland Forum (a Conference of nationalist parties north and south, meeting in Dublin between May 1983 and May 1984) has been for some sort of federal arrangement. The Anglo-Irish Agreement provides for joint authority in embryo, but that has never been an end in itself. The Agreement is more important as process than as 'solution', and shall be scrapped when permanent institutions of governance can be fashioned. According to Padraig O'Malley, the SDLP position may be distilled thus:

> An autonomous Northern Ireland state within a federal Ireland and an Anglo-Irish Council providing the institutional link with Britain, which would provide for British citizenship. An agreement along these lines would then be put to the people of the North *and* the people of the South in two separate referenda; to become binding, it would have to be ratified in both jurisdictions.[6]

Perhaps there is a Heath-Robinson quality to this machinery. That is only because it is designed to accommodate a jumble of cultural identities, not all compatible. One thing at least is plain, that constitutional nationalist thinking has gone beyond the simple anti-partitionism of the past, and in spite of challenge from Sinn Fein has done so without loss of face. This achievement deserves recognition.

PROVISIONAL SINN FEIN

The SDLP has consistently opposed use of violence for political purposes. Provisional Sinn Fein makes no such repudiation. Formed in 1970 as the political voice of the Provisional IRA, it has embraced 'armed struggle' as the means of forcing British withdrawal. Latterly it has also entered the electoral arena, challenging the SDLP for nationalist votes and embarrassing those who claimed that it feared the normal tests of legitimacy. This strategy of 'a ballot paper in one hand, an Armalite in the other' has reaped dividends, for Sinn Fein if for few else. The party now has a presence in local government, and between 1983 and 1992 its president, Gerry Adams, was abstentionist MP for West Belfast. On the other hand, its support has dipped since the mid 1980s and it has never polled well in the Irish Republic. Its vote in Northern Ireland elections now seems to hover around 11 per cent of the total, compared to the SDLP's 20 per cent.

Does this mean that a sizeable minority within the nationalist community supports the IRA? Not necessarily. Sinn Fein itself argues that a vote for one does not imply support for the other. This is a posture to preserve claims to democratic legitimacy, but there is some truth to it. Part of Sinn Fein's appeal is to the unemployed working class, also to hard core nationalists disillusioned with the SDLP. Nevertheless, there is no denying that some of the party's support represents straight-forward sanction of the IRA.

The association with paramilitarism has made Sinn Fein politically untouchable. (This is almost literally so: consider the fuss when Irish President Mary Robinson shook Gerry Adams' hand on a visit to Belfast in June 1993.) Until it renounces violence, it shall be excluded from negotiation by unionists, SDLP, the British and Irish governments and the Churches. The party seems unmoved. Sinn Fein continues to believes that the strategy of ballot and bullet has worked. Without it, there would have been no Anglo-Irish Agreement (an odd boast from a party which opposes same). Moreover, violence is a necessary preliminary to negotiation. 'You may be able to bomb and shoot a British connection out of existence,' argues Gerry Adams, the language supposedly conciliatory, but thereafter creative politicians must take over. No-one save Adams and his party seems persuaded by this logic.

Unionist loathing of Sinn Fein is naturally deep, but so also is that of the SDLP. The latter has witnessed first hand the consequences for the minority of continuing violence. Consider John Hume's observation of August 1989:

> The Provisional IRA and other Republican groups have killed six times more people than have the British Army. They have killed two

and a half times more Catholics than the British Army, the RUC and the UDR put together, and in the last ten years have even killed more Catholics than the loyalist paramilitaries. Somewhere along the road defending the Catholic community seems to have been lost sight of.[7]

Sinn Fein has yet to provide a convincing answer.

NOTES

1 Moloney and Pollak, op cit, p.269.
2 Quoted in D McKittrick, *Despatches from Belfast* (Blackstaff Press, Belfast, 1989), p.59.
3 cf. C Smyth, *Ian Paisley: Voice of Protestant Ulster* (Scottish Academic Press, Edinburgh, 1987), p.135.
4 P O'Malley, *Northern Ireland: Questions of Nuance* (Blackstaff Press, Belfast, 1990), p.19.
5 Ibid, p.21.
6 Ibid, p.24.
7 Gaffikin and Morrissey, op cit, p.32.

7 THE INTERNATIONAL DIMENSION

Northern Ireland's problems have more than local context. They impinge on the European Community and have been a source of concern in British-American relations. (To a lesser degree the affairs of the province are followed in other places: Australia has a substantial Irish Catholic population, Canada a sizeable number of Orangemen.) Optimists see opportunity here, thinking that international politics may yield solutions which have proved elusive in a national sphere. Pessimists believe that provincial bigots like nothing better than to parade themselves on a world stage. Somewhere between lies a core of realism which recognises that, almost unwittingly, Northern Ireland has had to change as global structures have changed. Even Ulster may be affected by that grandiose creation of recent times, the 'new world order'. It can hardly avoid it.

THE EUROPEAN CONTEXT

As part of the United Kingdom, Northern Ireland has enjoyed membership of the EC since 1973. The Republic of Ireland joined the Community in the same year. Since the coming into operation of the single European market on 1 January 1993 trade barriers between member states have been lifted, along with work restrictions and the like. Regulations governing goods and services are being standardised. A European currency of sorts exists, also a passport. Brussels has thus achieved what Belfast, London and Dublin never attempted: the border has become an economic irrelevance. Nationalists imagine that Europe may make it a political irrelevance also. Of the ironies of the Irish question, this is one of the richest: those once wedded to nation-state now rest their hopes in European federalism.

Within the EC, Northern Ireland is one of the most deprived of all 68 regions (Table 7.1, overleaf). It is also by some distance the poorest of all UK regions, closest to it being Wales (83.7) and the north of England (86.9). The Republic of Ireland (which for EC purposes counts as both a nation and a region) is one of the small number of EC regions that is poorer. In consequence, Northern Ireland – like the Republic – has been a substantial beneficiary of Community funds. In addition to the price-support mechanism of the Common Agricultural Policy (invaluable in an area where farming remains a major activity) there has been heavy additional expenditure to tackle the specific problems of regionality and industrial underdevelopment, with smaller sums also devoted to the enhancement of community relations. In 1985-86, for example, the gain to Northern Ireland was £84 million. In July 1993 it was announced that the province would receive a total of £1.04 billion in structural funds over the following six years.

Table 7.1 Poorest EC regions, 1990

	GDP[1]
	EC12=100
Nisia (Greece)	44.6
Kentriki Ellada (Greece)	44.7
Voreia Ellada (Greece)	46.2
Attiki (Greece)	50.4
Portugal	56.2
Southern Spain	59.1
Central Spain	62.3
Northeast Spain	62.7
Sicily	66.3
Ireland	68.2
Southern Italy	69.1
Campania (Italy)	69.3
Sardinia	73.5
Northern Ireland	**74.3**

1 Gross domestic product per head at market prices converted into purchasing power standards
Source Statistical Office of the European Communities

However, largesse does not always translate into political affection. Of Northern Ireland's three Euro-MPs, only one, Hume (SDLP), has been an enthusiast for the European ideal. His colleagues, Ian Paisley (DUP) and John Taylor (OUP), have garnered votes on opposition to Brussels, while never refusing its money. Paisley has been skilful in squeezing revenue from an institution he claims to despise, though attempts to use the European Parliament as a soap-box – he was ejected from the chamber for heckling the Pope, for example – have embarrassed even the home crowd. To those unversed in evangelical fundamentalism (even to some initiates) Paisley's attitude to the community seems unhinged. 'What holds the Common Market together?'

he asked in 1984. 'Satanic power.' How else could so many 'diverse nations with so many problems, so many difficulties, so many political, economic and military strains ... suddenly come together?' Denouncing the 'greatest Roman Catholic super-state the world has ever known', he has continued to draw a generous salary as Euro-MP since 1979.[2]

The bluster is for local, perhaps even personal, consumption. Behind the scenes Paisley and Hume have been adept at milking the Common Market, often to the benefit of farmers. Europe has thus provided an arena where Northern Ireland politicians can cooperate to mutual advantage. If not in Belfast, then in Brussels, power-sharing has acquired a shadowy reality.

When deeper designs are perceived this harmony vanishes. Hume has never disguised his belief that Europe may provide structures towards a settlement in Northern Ireland and he has proved more active than others in building alliances to that end. The result has been a series of modest political victories: in 1984 the European Parliament adopted a report which called for power-sharing, in 1985 it endorsed the Anglo-Irish Agreement. Unionists reacted predictably. Interference in domestic politics is not to their taste – unless, naturally, the interference is along unionist lines.

The EC is likely, then, to play a greater economic than political role in Northern Ireland's affairs, if only because its parliament (little respected anyway) lends itself too easily to posture and gesture. But the former is not to be despised. Terrorism feeds on poverty and is itself a cause of it. Moreover, economic integration of any kind can only reinforce a sense of the irrationality of 'armed struggle' in a world of expanding markets. Quasi-federalism may yet prove a partial solvent of ancient antagonisms.

THE UNITED STATES

Some 20 million Americans claim Irish lineage. This represents a sizeable lobby in a political culture where the lobby is king. It also represents a bloc which although not unitary, and probably more powerful in local than national elections, is nevertheless better informed than most. As the *New York Times* editorialised on St Patrick's Day, 1981, 'in a real sense, the violence that scars a distant land has become local news'.[3] Insofar as it has political and not simply cultural identity, Irish America is largely but not entirely nationalist in sympathy. As a factor in US foreign policy it is not nearly as important as (say) the Jewish vote. All the same, successive administrations have interested themselves in Irish matters, and Irish politicians have assiduously courted the Americans. Usually this has borne fruit in predictable ways: a certain greenness of rhetoric before elections, sentimental platitudes afterwards. On occasion, however, the American connection has been genuinely significant.

In the sea-change of 1980 Irish Americans, historically Democrat, shifted in numbers to the Republican Party. Another change may also be noticed. A lobby previously inclined to sentimental endorsement of the 'armed struggle' showed signs of new maturity. Consider the establishment of the Friends of Ireland in 1981. This group, sponsored by 24 leading senators and congressmen, represented an open challenge to the Ad Hoc Congressional Committee for Irish Affairs, which at that time was Irish-America's chief political vehicle. The Committee was controlled by Congressman Mario Biaggi, an old-time New York street politician, who had somehow never found the words to condemn political violence in Ireland. The Friends of Ireland by contrast opposed terrorism in favour of Irish reunification by consent 'with full safeguards for the rights of 'both sections of the community'.[4]

The capture of Irish-American support notwithstanding, the Reagan years did not see a greening of the White House. Other priorities existed, not least a desire to fight international terrorism, in which the IRA was believed to be implicated. Reagan's first Irish statement as president called on Americans to ensure that well-intended contributions did not 'end up in the hands of those who perpetuate violence'.[5] Twice in his first year in office, he disavowed Irish unity as an aim of US foreign policy, preferring to emphasise the need for an internal Northern Ireland solution. In other words, his ideas were tailored to please Margaret Thatcher more than Irish America. Later he displayed greater warmth towards an 'Irish dimension'. On his sentimental (and electorally calculating) visit to Ireland in 1984, he confined himself to platitude.

1985 also saw the Anglo-Irish Agreement, which Reagan warmly supported. This pleased Thatcher, also most of the Irish lobby; a rare double. After its signing, an International Fund for Ireland was established, with Reagan's blessing. In its first three years, the fund contributed $120 million to economic projects in Northern Ireland and in border areas.

Bush continued the policy of deference to British wishes on Ireland. He urged Americans not to donate to the Irish Northern Aid Committee (Noraid), a channel of funding for paramilitaries and their agents. Funds fell away, though probably for other reasons. (The hunger strikes of 1981 were good for Noraid's business, the Anglo-Irish Agreement bad.) Ireland was not a priority, even for a foreign-policy president.

President Clinton as candidate courted the Irish-American vote more energetically than had his two predecessors. He promised if elected to send a peace envoy to Ireland and to support Gerry Adams's applica-tion for a visitor's visa to enter the United States; neither idea has been heard of since. Clinton received Irish-American votes, but mainly for reasons unrelated to Ireland. In office previous policy was contin-ued, with nods from time to time in the direction of human rights.

Does any of this matter? Some practical consequences have flowed from American interest in Ireland. Unionists maintain that the involve-ment is powered by old-fashioned nationalism of the sort represented by the Irish National Caucus. They point to the 'MacBride Principles', which urge US companies not to deal with Northern Ireland firms deemed to discriminate against Catholics. After vigorous lobbying, the principles were written into law by several states in the late Eighties. However, successive Federal Administrations have opposed 'MacBride', as have all parties in Northern Ireland except Sinn Fein. The SDLP has been especially critical. Anti-discrimination legislation was indeed strengthened in 1988 as a result of the Caucus campaign. But lost investment has also resulted. For some Irish Americans, the principle seems to be that no jobs are better than 'unfair' ones. Northern Ireland itself can ill afford such scruples.

NOTES

1 Moloney and Pollak, op cit, p.406.
2 *New York Times*, 17 March 1981.
3 *New York Times*, 18 March 1981.
4 Ibid.

8 TERRORISM AND SECURITY

An illness which proves resistant to treatment may either be misdiagnosed or incurable. So far we have considered remedies – power-sharing, a Council of Ireland, the Anglo-Irish Agreement – which assume that the Northern Ireland 'problem' is at root political. They do not seem to have worked. After a quarter-century of violence, the body count continues. There is an alternative view, usually but not exclusively expressed by unionist politicians: that the answer to the current conflict lies in tighter security. Chronic lawlessness and ideologically motivated gangsterism can only be cured, so the argument goes, by vigorous policing and an efficient justice system. Civil rights must come second, and political initiatives a distant third. The sorry history of initiatives seems to justify their impatience: but is the demand for tougher action much more than swagger and emotionalism?

THE PARAMILITARY CULTURE

The emotional appeal of 'rooting out the terrorists' should not conceal the difficulty of the task. Both republican and loyalist paramilitaries are well-entrenched in their respective areas, are substantially supplied with sophisticated weaponry, and have largely resisted infiltration by counter-intelligence. Arms shipments from Libya in the mid 1980s have given the IRA a base from which to continue its activities well into the 1990s. The explosive material semtex is light, easily concealed and deadly. The organisation remains 'armed to the teeth'.[1]

Loyalists too have recently shown a harder face. Their preferred weapon is assassination, of IRA members or their presumed supporters; occasionally, in factional fighting, of their own kind. In March 1993 the killing of four Catholic workmen gave notice that Protestant paramilitarism is far from dormant. Its chief engines are the Ulster Defence Association and the Ulster Volunteer Force, both illegal, though the former only since 1992. The UDA has had occasional political pretensions, but for the most part it remains a shadowy army of Protestant defence. The major claim of the UVF is responsibility for some of Ulster's grisliest sectarian killings. Total terrorist-related deaths in the period since 1969 now total more than 3000 (Table 8.1).

Injuries total almost 40 000. In a province of 1.6 million inhabitants, these are big numbers.

Table 8.1 Terrorist-related deaths in Northern Ireland, 1969-92

	RUC	RUCR	Army	UDR	Civilians	Total
1969	1	0	0	0	12	13
1970	2	0	0	0	23	25
1971	11	0	43	5	115	174
1972	14	3	103	26	321	467
1973	10	3	58	8	171	250
1974	12	3	28	7	166	216
1975	7	4	14	6	216	247
1976	13	10	14	15	245	297
1977	8	6	15	14	69	112
1978	4	6	14	7	50	81
1979	9	5	38	10	51	113
1980	3	6	8	9	50	76
1981	13	8	10	13	57	101
1982	8	4	21	7	57	97
1983	9	9	5	10	44	77
1984	7	2	9	10	36	64
1985	14	9	2	4	25	54
1986	10	2	4	8	37	61
1987	9	7	3	8	66	93
1988	4	2	21	12	54	93
1989	7	2	12	2	39	62
1990	7	5	7	8	49	76
1991	5	1	5	8	75	94
1992	2	1	3	0	78	84
Total	**189**	**98**	**437**	**197**	**2104**	**3028**

Note Figures for civilians include terrorist suspects and prison officers
Source Northern Ireland Office

The IRA shall attempt to avoid disasters such as the Enniskillen bombing (1987) and the deaths of children in Warrington (1993): but public outrage alone shall not stop it. Indeed, when anger turns to defeatism, the terrorists' task is nearly complete. Bombing key targets in Britain and the Republic of Ireland is central to this strategy. Attacks on the Conservative Party Conference at Brighton (1984) – five died, others were crippled – and on Downing Street (1991) showed a capacity to penetrate the tightest security. An explosion in the City of London (April 1993) caused massive financial loss, also loss of nerve. In July 1993 a 'ring of steel' was placed around London's financial district; in all likelihood, an invitation for the IRA to try again. Total terrorist-related deaths since 1969 in Britain, the Republic and Europe are shown in Table 8.2.

Table 8.2 Terrorist-related deaths in Britain, the Republic of Ireland and Europe, 1969-92

	Britain	**Republic**	**Europe**	**Total**
1969	0	0	0	0
1970	0	3	0	3
1971	0	3	0	3
1972	7	4	0	11
1973	2	6	0	8
1974	45	37	0	82
1975	10	7	0	17
1976	2	4	0	6
1977	0	4	0	4
1978	0	1	0	1
1979	1	6	2	9
1980	0	4	2	6
1981	3	1	0	4
1982	11	2	0	13
1983	6	4	0	10
1984	5	1	0	6
1985	0	4	0	4
1986	0	0	0	0
1987	0	6	0	6
1988	1	1	7	9
1989	11	1	4	16
1990	3	0	3	6
1991	3	0	0	3
1992	6	0	0	6
Total	**116**	**100**	**18**	**234**

Source Northern Ireland Office

Paramilitary groups are well supplied with intelligence. Nor do they lack money. Systematic fraud and racketeering have yielded high returns for both IRA and UDA, each lord of its own domain. Estimates of the IRA's income vary, but it is certainly several millions of pounds annually. The IRA, in short, is a major foe, its members carefully recruited and trained. Moreover, unlike some other terrorist groups, it has the advantage of fighting for an achievable goal. This permits the long view: in five, ten, or 15 years, the IRA reckons, Britain shall simply tire of fighting an unwinnable war, and withdraw.

Social collapse and a culture of terrorism have resulted. In these circumstances it is simplistic to speak of 'rooting out terrorists'. 'I was born and bred in rioting,' boasted a Belfast ten year old to a visiting American in 1982. Most of the ten-year-old's friends had 'never known a time when rioting, shooting, bombing, assassination, knee-capping, arrests, dawn raids, and feuds between paramilitary groups were not 'part of their environment'.[2] Those who wish to extirpate terrorism must first convince local populations that *their* authority is to be preferred over that of the terrorist. In the ghettoes support for Provoism may oscillate and occasionally disappear: it has yet to be replaced by enthusiasm for the established forces of law and order.

LAW AND ORDER

Policing in these circumstances requires a mixture of toughness and tact. Likewise the legal system must perform its usual task – to render fair judgment without compromising the claims of individual or com-munity – in a highly unusual world. Jury trial in terrorist cases has been suspended since 1973. Instead, a High Court or County Court judge hears the case, who then must explain his verdict in writing. These 'Diplock Courts', intended to guard against intimidation of jurors, have mostly worked well. Their critics condemn not the absence of a jury but the fact that only one judge sits. Against this civil libertarian argument is the criticism that the Diplock system does not 'work' because in certain well-publicised 'supergrass' trials, acquit-tals have been returned. This claim is weak. It is not the function of the courts to presume guilt. Moreover, these cases turned on ques-tions of evidence – the admissibility of uncorroborated testimony of paid informers – which would have been decisive in jury trial also.

In the 1980s the RUC worked strenuously to improve its reputation in the nationalist community, with some success. (The sight of police-men under attack from loyalists enraged by the Anglo-Irish Agree-ment may have helped.) However, serious doubts remain. The 'Stalker Affair' was a public relations disaster. Six unarmed Catholics suspected of terrorist intent were shot dead by police in South Armagh in 1982. Appointed to investigate, John Stalker, deputy Chief Constable of Manchester, found his inquiries impeded by senior police officers, and was eventually removed from the case. Sir Patrick Mayhew, then Attorney General, later conceded that the shootings perverted the course of justice, but declined to prosecute on national security grounds, arguing that intelligence networks would be compromised. (Sir Patrick became Northern Ireland Secretary in 1992.) Stalker also argued against prosecution, for different reasons: the real culprits were not the officers who fired but those who gave the orders. 'The RUC has tried hard to shed its sectarian image,' he drily wrote, 'but the publicity surrounding this investigation was a set-back.'[3]

Nor has confidence in the judiciary recovered from the case of the 'Birmingham Six'. The convictions of six Irishmen for the Birmingham pub bombings (1974) had been subject to sustained public criticism when Home Secretary Douglas Hurd referred them to the Court of Appeal in 1988. They were nevertheless upheld. A further appeal (1991) quashed the convictions – which may perhaps represent final vindication of a sort for the court system. From beginning to end, the episode seemed to place the 'system', not the Irishmen, in the dock. Stories of doctored evidence and judicial intransigence shall be the stuff of nationalist myth for years to come.

ARMY INTELLIGENCE

'Rooting out the terrorists' may therefore be counterproductive. It may also assume undue faith in army intelligence. Conventional wisdom holds that most paramilitaries are well known to the police and that only pusillanimity prevents their seizure. Yet informers have not always yielded reliable results, and undercover agents may themselves have been involved in terrorist activity. Too often, it seems, information is simply lacking or, when gathered, improperly understood.

Consider two cases. In 1989 a loyalist gunman, Michael Stone, was convicted of the killings of three people at an IRA funeral in Belfast. In court it became apparent that he had been an active assassin for several years and that he had links with at least three paramilitary groups. A one-man killing machine, he had stalked republicans all over Northern Ireland, picking off his targets with planning and precision. Yet the police had last encountered him in 1977, when he was in trouble for little more 'than hooliganism'.[4]

Consider also the case of the gun-running ship *Eksund*. Here was an intelligence lapse of astonishing proportions, its consequences likely to be felt for years. French customs officials intercepted the trawler *Eksund* off the Brittany coast in November 1987. Expecting drugs, they discovered instead a huge arsenal: machine guns, rocket launchers, surface-to-air missiles, two tons of Semtex, 1000 Kalashnikov rifles, 50 tons of ammunition. The ship had come from Libya. But the coup turned sour. British and Irish intelligence refused to accept that the arms were bound for the IRA. Almost willing themselves to disbelieve the worst, they claimed that the IRA had no links with Libya, and that they had no need of such a large cache. Nor was this the final false inference. As David McKittrick writes,

> Even when it emerged that the trawler was crewed by five Irishmen, the RUC and Gardai attempted to cling to the theory that they had been acting for some foreign terrorist grouping. Only when it was established that three of them were known IRA members did the unpalatable truth sink home.[5]

Although the ship was seized, previous consignments had entered Ireland quite undetected. These episodes may be isolated, but they ought to weaken assumptions of police and army omniscience. Big Brother may be watching, but often with a squint.

Tighter security is not, for all that, impossible. Calls for the reintroduction of internment, an occasional unionist cry, have been echoed by some commentators, even in quarters in the Irish Republic. There is little likelihood of it. Tougher sentencing might have greater chance of success. On its own of course it could achieve little. Combined with sustained action against racketeering and efforts to encourage confidence in the police, it may go some way towards eradication of the paramilitary culture. However, to combine carrot and stick in this way runs the perennial risk of creating ghetto heroes. Concentration on security has its place, but in the end the problem of Northern Ireland remains one of politics, not policing.

NOTES

1 McKittrick, op cit, p.130.
2 J Sluka, *Hearts and Minds, Water and Fish: Support for the IRA and INLA in a Northern Ireland Ghetto* (JAI Press, Greenwich CT, 1989), p.275.
3 J Stalker, *Stalker* (Harrap, London, 1988), p.255.
4 McKittrick, op cit.
5 Ibid, p.82.

9 POLITICS AFTER 1985

The Anglo-Irish Agreement was a watershed. It seemed to catch unionists off guard while providing a boost for constitutional nationalism. Though the immediate results were mixed, its framers sought to induce, in the longer term, changes of attitude in the Northern Ireland parties, and people. This chapter considers the success or otherwise of that strategy.

UNIONIST OPPOSITION TO HILLSBOROUGH

Addressing the Dail in December 1985, Garret Fitzgerald expressed regret that the Anglo-Irish Agreement had 'yet to be fully appreciated by Unionists'. This was understatement. The indignation of Northern Protestants knew few bounds: a 'cold fury', James Molyneaux called it, such as he had not seen in 40 years of political life. In another sense, though, Fitzgerald's observation was wrong. Unionists appreciated the Agreement only too well, seeing it as the end of the union and of their own local hegemony.

The intuition (not exclusive to unionists) that the Agreement represented a pious fraud was sound. The Thatcher-Fitzgerald document could only work by being all things to all men: to unionists a bulwark of the union, to nationalists a quasi-juridical forum for the expression of non-British identity, to the respective governments an affirmation of separate but legitimate interests in the north of Ireland.

So delicate a fiction needed diplomacy in the selling. It was not always apparent. Shortly after the Agreement came into force Secretary of State Tom King commended it to unionists on the ground that Dublin had accepted partition 'in perpetuity'. This was precisely what Dublin had not accepted. Fitzgerald called the remarks 'inappropriate and inaccurate'. King apologised the next day.

The Agreement was indeed juridically ambiguous, but it had a political clarity which few could doubt. Mary Holland, a veteran commentator on Irish affairs, captured it:

Whatever happens to the Anglo-Irish Agreement, and nobody doubts there are extremely bumpy times ahead, Northern nationalists know that things will never be the same again. After Sunningdale it became unthinkable for the SDLP to accept less than power-sharing at government level. So now, even if the deal goes wrong, a British government has accepted that Northern Catholics are Irish people who have a right to have their interests represented by the Irish government.[1]

It was this incremental quality which so exercised unionists. They feared that if the Agreement were not quickly reversed things would indeed never be the same again. A system of joint authority could soon crystallise into permanence.

Unionist discomfort was heightened by suggestions that they had nobody to blame for their troubles but themselves. Nationalist gloating was never far from the surface. The systematic exclusion of the minority from government, before and after 1969, had brought them to this pass. Unionists, it was said, never missed an opportunity to miss an opportunity: not a bad summary, in fact, of several centuries of history. Witness the failed chances to lessen nationalist alienation – power-sharing, the Convention, the Atkins talks, rolling devolution. It was a damning inventory. The Agreement seemed to say that if unionists could not seize their chances, others would have to seize them on their behalf.

The importance of Hillsborough, then, was that it represented a significant opportunity for unionist self-examination. As we saw in Chapter 4, however, initial reaction was all grand gesture and showy moral certainty – mass resignations from Westminster, by-election victories, a Day of Action, withdrawal from local councils, an 'Ulster Says No' poster campaign. Some of this had a sinister accompaniment. The Day of Action (3 March 1986) was violent, and it prompted King to accuse Paisley of trouble-making. Sir John Hermon, Chief Constable of the RUC, spoke of unidentified politicians 'consorting with paramilitary elements'. But for unionists the ominous feature of the campaign was its result. It simply did not work.

AN END TO DRIFT?: 1987

It took some time for this to dawn. Moderate unionists urged talks – but outside the framework of the Agreement. This was the perennial refrain: suspension of Hillsborough first, talks later. Others doubted the wisdom even of talks. Not until early 1987 was it realised that bluster alone had failed. Paisley and Molyneaux therefore appointed a Task Force to consider the way forward. Consisting of three senior politicians – Harold McCusker and Frank Millar (both OUP), Peter Robinson (DUP) – this was the first evidence of serious self-assessment since the signing of the Agreement. Its report, *An End to Drift*, was published in July 1987. This was a commendably honest document. In it, distaste for the Agreement was undisguised – the line remained that it had fundamentally altered the union, that it would lead to a united Ireland, and that it should be scrapped – but acknowledgement was also made of the inadequacy of opposition alone. What then to put in its place? Three options were presented: return to devolved government, independence, full integration into the United Kingdom. There was no 'Irish dimension'.

The authors recognised that there was 'substantial support' for the third option, but warned that 'the Whitehall establishment' was strongly opposed to it. That left two, each feasible but one better than the other:

> Devolved government is therefore our objective and whilst we hope this will prove attainable within the context of the United Kingdom, Unionists would be wise and prudent to anticipate that it might not.

It was a cautious report, cautiously welcomed. Only crusading integrationists attacked it.

An End to Drift did not however end the drift. Its central proposal – talks with the British government with the aim of restoring a devolved administration – required prior ending of the Hillsborough accord. But this was unacceptable to both governments, also to the SDLP. As a result an odd unreality descended over politics. Unionists believed that drift was over simply because they had pronounced it so, and (another delusion) that the Agreement was unworkable because they had refused to work with it. The Conference continued its work regardless, oddly removed from all the anguish.

Protestant vulnerability was powerfully symbolised by the poppy day bombing at Enniskillen in November 1987 which killed 11 people, injured many more. Yet that tragedy in another sense strengthened the unionist position. Revulsion at IRA tactics galvanised opinion

North and South, enabling the Dublin government (under Charles Haughey) to continue its tough anti-terrorist stance. Moreover, a massacre on Remembrance Sunday altered opinion in Britain. Until then, the assorted trappings of loyalism – Union Jacks, pictures of the Queen, extravagant assertions of Britishness – looked overdone. In a perverse way they seemed, to the English, typically Irish behaviour. But Enniskillen revealed a people not factitiously British, who (like their war dead) deserved respect. They also deserved support. After the bombing, polls showed for the first time a majority of opinion in favour of *keeping* troops in Northern Ireland. This did not last long, but for a time it reinforced unionist determination not to yield.

TWO INITIATIVES: 1988

Yet resilience can become principled immobility. Commentators thought they saw hopeful glimmers at the end of 1987, but 1988 brought few achievements. According to the *Irish Times*, it was 'the year that politics stood still'.[2] There were only two developments of note: an initiative on the loyalist side, and one on the nationalist.

In January 1988, unionist leaders presented Secretary of State King with proposals for administrative devolution. The same month, John Hume met Gerry Adams for talks. The Paisley-Molyneaux plan was for a system of committees corresponding to existing departments – agriculture, economic development, and the like – which would be answerable to a new Stormont assembly. Chairmanships would be allocated proportionate to strength in the assembly, which would allow nationalists some responsibility. It was a modest proposal – too modest for nationalists – and it seemed to die of anaemia.

The Hume-Adams talks were just as modest (both denied that a cease-fire was on the agenda) but predictably sparked an angry reaction. Hume, architect and builder of the Anglo-Irish Agreement, stood low in unionist eyes. Talks with Sinn Fein lowered him further. He made no apology, but the talks got nowhere. Hume attempted to persuade Adams of the SDLP's new article of faith: that the Agreement proved Britain's neutrality as far as the constitutional status of Northern Ireland was concerned, and that the 'armed struggle' was therefore both pointless and counter-productive. Adams demurred. He saw no evidence of neutrality in massive physical force. The discussions petered out in August. When they ended, Hume began a series of strong denunciations of Sinn Fein, culminating at the party conference in November with an attack on its 'fascist' tendencies.

NATIONALIST POLITICS AFTER 1985: THE SDLP

Nationalist politics after Hillsborough did not experience the anguish or urgency that afflicted unionism, but important challenges still had to be faced. Both its elements were playing a longer game: the SDLP waiting for the Anglo-Irish Agreement to 'work', Sinn Fein waiting for it to fail. Each was also waiting and working for the other to lose ground among Northern Irish Catholics. Support for the SDLP was substantial but still vulnerable to Sinn Fein erosion – one reason for the negotiation of the Agreement in the first place. Hillsborough altered profoundly the dynamic of nationalist debate. If the Anglo-Irish Agreement could be made to succeed – or at least not fail – then constitutional nationalism had a future. Were it not to work, Sinn Fein would have a powerful argument against reliance on conventional politics alone as a means towards nationalist ends.

Though not a creature of its leader, the SDLP closely reflected John Hume's thinking on most matters. Indeed when some members resigned rather than accept the Anglo-Irish Agreement, his hold on the party became even firmer. There was good reason for this: Hume's thinking was subtle and impressive, and the party was lucky to have him. From mixed materials he had fashioned a coherent political body – moderate on the 'constitutional' question, left-of-centre on social and economic matters. Unionist critics were probably insufficiently grateful for its existence. Their own position would have been much more exposed without the presence of a channel which allowed the minority to express peaceful disenchantment with the northern state.

Hume's task after 1985 was to sell Hillsborough, and he executed it with skill. The performance was the more impressive for his having to sell it to two different audiences: nationalists and unionists, indeed two sets of nationalists – those north of the border, and those south, neither agreed on strategy or even the meaning of Irish 'unification'. Northern nationalists had to be assured that the Agreement would make a difference in their lives; southern nationalists had to be assured that it did not make partition permanent; unionists had to be persuaded that it posed no threat to their way of life. That Hume could make these claims and still appear sincere was a tribute (depending on taste) to his powers of analysis or of self-delusion.

His first difficulty lay with Charles Haughey's Fianna Fail party. In 1986, from the safety of opposition, Fianna Fail launched a series of attacks on the Agreement in language hard to distinguish from that of Sinn Fein. Haughey expressed the standard republican criticism: that the Irish government had accepted 'British sovereignty over part of Ireland [and] will involve itself in assisting and advising the British government to rule that part of Ireland more effectively'. This seemed carping to Hume. For a time the two parties were scarcely on speaking terms. No senior Fianna Fail visitor attended the SDLP annual conference in 1986, nor did the party send a message of goodwill. Hume used the occasion to urge nationalist 'solidarity of approach' to the Agreement, an implied reproach to the senior republican party.

That conference was a good illustration of the difficulties facing a moderate nationalist party in the aftermath of the Agreement. It was no simple task to mollify both Charles Haughey and Ian Paisley, while convincing one's own supporters that moderate nationalism meant more than splitting the difference. Some questioned the value of mollifying Paisley in the first place. Seamus Mallon, deputy leader of the party, cheered delegates by mocking Paisley and Molyneaux for their inarticulacy in the face of the Agreement. Hume showed greater restraint, but in essence his argument was the same – that Hillsborough *had* weakened unionists and that this was in the unionists' best interests. Their veto on political progress was gone. Hume promoted a pluralist vision of Ireland's identities as mutually inclusive. Lasting peace would only come about through such mutuality and (for the time being) only the Agreement enshrined it.

NATIONALIST POLITICS AFTER 1985: SINN FEIN

Sinn Fein meanwhile continued with a pluralism of its own: politics and physical force. The many contradictions of this 'armalite and ballot box' policy did not bother either party leadership or faithful. How did they justify, for example, a mandate for 'armed struggle' when Sinn Fein received only 12 per cent of the vote in Northern Ireland and scarcely 2 per cent in the Republic? The standard reply was that the British presence was mandate enough. This was strange logic. Equally curious was the party's attitude to democratic institutions. In 1986 it ended its policy of refusing, if elected, to take seats in Dail Eireann, the Republic's parliament. It continued its abstention from Westminster. Thus in the jurisdiction where it *had* won a seat (Gerry Adams was MP for West Belfast between 1983 and 1992) it abstained, and where it had no chance of winning it was prepared to sit. Either way, elections were not a priority.

Above all, Sinn Fein could never make a convincing case that it respected the views of northern Protestants. Adams, addressing the party's annual conference in 1987, acknowledged the 'great trauma' that Irish unification would present for unionists. 'We offer them a settlement based on throwing in their lot with the rest of the Irish people and ending sectarianism. We offer them peace.' The overture was hollow: he ended by paying tribute to two IRA men recently killed by their own bomb.

Notice, in short, the oddity of politics after 1985. Sinn Fein pretended to embrace unionists and reserved its greatest venom for the SDLP. It condemned the 'nightmare' of the Anglo-Irish Agreement – as did unionists. It offered peace to northern Protestants by offering them war. The reaction of most outsiders was probably weary bafflement.

NATIONALISM: THE POLITICS OF PLURALISM

Hume's pluralism invited debate whereas Adams' invited debate to cease. At times, however, the SDLP leader gave the impression of regarding dialogue as an end in itself – proof that each side *was* capable of mutual respect. But to talk of accommodation of different traditions was not of itself to bring that accommodation into being. At issue was not the legitimate existence of separate identities in Ireland but the constitutional structure by which each could flourish. For the SDLP a nationalism of cultural conquest – of Protestantism – was unacceptable. This concealed a problem. For many northerners it was precisely the link with Britain which gave fullest expression to their Protestantism. British liberty, they held, was the liberty to be Protestant – or Catholic, for that matter. Thus the SDLP's invitation to enter a pluralist Ireland was answered by an invitation to make the most of a pluralist Britain. Each side proclaimed itself 'more pluralist than thou' and as a result both remained as far apart as ever.

The heart of the matter was a question of trust. In spite of his reasonableness – perhaps because of it – Hume was a suspicious figure to unionists. They saw themselves trapped in his web of words as he threatened to achieve by euphemism what Sinn Fein hoped to achieve by force. An 'agreed Ireland', an Ireland of 'unity through diversity', an Ireland for 'Catholic, Protestant, and Dissenter': to unionists these were the old hegemonic designs dressed up in new linguistic finery. Why not, they asked, have all this splendid cultural co-mingling – within Britain?

Table 9.1 Westminster general election results in Northern Ireland, 1983-92

	1983		1987		1992	
	Vote	Seats	Vote	Seats	Vote	Seats
Ulster Unionists	34.0	11	37.8	9	34.5	9
Democratic Unionists	20.0	3	11.7	3	13.1	3
SDLP	17.9	1	21.1	3	23.5	4
Sinn Fein	13.4	1	11.4	1	10.0	0
Alliance	8.0	0	10.0	0	8.7	0
Popular Unionists	3.0	1	2.5	1	2.5	1

If Hume found unionists hard to persuade, nationalists proved easier. The SDLP/Sinn Fein rivalry for Catholic support was resolved in favour of the former in the period after Hillsborough. In the 1986 Westminster by-elections, the parties faced each other in four seats, with the SDLP vote rising by 6 per cent and Sinn Fein's declining by 5.4 per cent. The general election of 1987 also saw an enhanced SDLP performance: its vote was up 3.2 per cent on 1983 to 21.1 per cent, whereas Sinn Fein's fell by 2 per cent to 11.4 per cent. A similar pattern was repeated at the 1992 general election (Table 9.1). This solid achievement was seized upon as vindication of the Agreement, no doubt with some measure of justice. On the other hand, Sinn Fein remained a locally formidable force, and it still commanded 35 per cent of the nationalist vote. The SDLP had little margin of error as it argued the case for a new Ireland.

NOTES

1 *Irish Times*, 4 December 1985.
2 *Irish Times*, 28 December 1988.

10 THE BROOKE INITIATIVE

Historians, with the advantage of perspective, often see long-term strategy where contemporaries only saw short-term opportunism. It is too early to speak of recent events in Northern Ireland in the light of history. Still, it is a fair bet that some later writers shall see the Anglo-Irish Agreement as a 'softening-up' exercise for what followed: the attempt by Peter Brooke, then Sir Patrick Mayhew, to resume political talks in the province. The pains taken by both to make a success of that task may lend credence to the view. Likewise the frequent insistence by John Major, Prime Minister from November 1990, on the need for dialogue. Paradoxically the patience of Major and his ministers may indicate that Britain's patience is at last running out.

BROOKE ARRIVES: 1989

'Is there intelligent life on Tom King?', asked writer and politician Conor Cruise O'Brien in the *Irish Times* in 1986. Apparently not, he concluded. Too often, in his early days in Northern Ireland, King appeared a disconnected object of dim and unsteady orbit, perhaps even a black hole from which no light at all could emerge. Yet after a poor start he survived to become the longest-serving Secretary of State, garnering handsome tributes when he left to become Defence Secretary in July 1989. Reform of the RUC, measures to end employment discrimination, improvement of cross-border security, job creation – they were all worthy achievements. On the other hand, political progress had been, in his own words, 'virtually non-existent'. Unionists never forgave Thatcher the Anglo-Irish Agreement, and they loathed her plenipotentiary for staunch support of it. As we have seen, the Agreement had permitted improvements in modest matters but it remained the greatest obstacle to advance on a wider scale.

King's replacement was Peter Brooke, chairman of the Conservative Party, whose family had Ulster connections going back several centuries. A Tory grandee of the old school, Brooke looked like a cut-price William Whitelaw without the latter's shrewdness. But it would have been wrong to underestimate him. He combined diplomatic suavity with frankness – a rare double. This might have been dangerous in a

Northern Ireland Secretary, whose task is to be all things to all men. But he also possessed a quality rarely exhibited by English politicians in Ireland: infinite patience.

The latter was his saving virtue. Brooke arrived in the province unburdened by high expectation. General pessimism pervaded the politics of Northern Ireland in 1989, though it took particular forms. Constitutional nationalists north and south of the border reluctantly accepted the status quo. They had reason for disappointment at the Anglo-Irish Agreement, but in the absence of anything better were inclined to stick with it. Loyalists were gloomy too. They thought themselves frozen out and recognised how their stock had fallen by failure to defeat the accord. It might have been easy for a new Secretary of State to allow these reciprocal sorrows to cancel each other out. Brooke reasoned however that the impasse could no longer be allowed to continue. The cost of inertia was too great in both financial and human terms.

A significant signal came from Peter Robinson (DUP), who declared that the 'political process' should resume. This marked the first major fissure in unionist unanimity since the Agreement. For their part, the OUP also saw the value of exploring new avenues. They thought for instance that the Irish Presidency of the European Community (January to June 1990) might offer a context in which they could make contact with Dublin without loss of face. Brooke's appointment marked a moment, then, when the new unionist realism (which commentators had been proclaiming for at least two years) might have borne fruit.

But what of Brooke himself? Early signs suggested that he saw his role as more than that of a consolidator. He was considerably more thoughtful than his predecessor in analysing the direction of British policy in Northern Ireland, and this included acknowledgement of previous mistakes. Like King, who began with a 'gaffe' – claiming that Dublin had accepted partition in perpetuity – Brooke's first foray seemed ill-judged. Unlike King's remark, however, he intended it. In November 1989 he incensed unionists by conceding that the IRA could not be defeated militarily. Honesty or idiocy? Unionists thought the latter. But the remark was not a slip of the tongue. It formed part of a larger syllogism. If the IRA could not be defeated by the army, Brooke argued, the army for its part could not be defeated by the IRA. Indefinite containment of one side by the other was self-evidently unsatisfactory. Moreover, economic improvement alone would not 'cause terrorism to falter'. The culture of alienation was too deeply ingrained for that. Some sort of initiative was therefore necessary to end an intolerable situation.

For a Tory of unionist sympathies, this was singular reasoning. It resembled Sinn Fein's reading of the Irish question more than that of any other party. For all that, Brooke was not in the business of rehabilitating Sinn Fein. Violence had to be renounced first, and there was as yet no sign of that. But he was attempting to make it easier for Sinn Fein to abandon the 'armed struggle' if that was its wish. He also gave out other signals – such as greater flexibility for parole of long-term republican prisoners – which suggested a willingness to make room for Sinn Fein to manoeuvre its supporters behind a more moderate position. Brooke understood something of political psychology. As with the unionist reluctance to speak to the Dublin government while the Anglo-Irish Agreement remained in place, the need to maintain face was the primary consideration. Progress would only be possible if each side to the conflict could move towards the centre without appearing to make concessions.

TALKS ABOUT TALKS: 1990

Brooke's initiative was a most modest affair. It involved not talks but 'talks about talks': an attempt to discover if sufficient common ground existed to make negotiations about devolution worthwhile. Even that proved problematic. Brooke began his conversations with the political parties in January 1990, and after ten months it appeared that common ground did not exist. A chronology of false hopes was enacted during that time.

What had gone wrong? First, unionists demanded that the Anglo-Irish Agreement be ended before the opening of any talks. How could a dialogue be conducted in good faith, they asked, with a damoclean sword over the head of one of the parties? The SDLP demanded that it should stay. It was by no means a final answer to the Irish question, they said, but it provided the basis for one. These positions were predictable and tactically inevitable. The SDLP had no intention of throwing away its best card before the bidding began. The unionists had no intention of conceding the permanence of the Agreement without a final fight. No-one can have been surprised that 'Hillsborough' was central to the early stages of 'talks about talks'.

But this was more than a procedural difficulty. The role of the Republic's government in any future talks mattered greatly to all parties because the very nature of those talks would be defined by it. For example, unionists wanted to talk to Dublin only when some structure of government had been agreed for Northern Ireland. The SDLP on the other hand hoped that unionists would meet Irish ministers *before* any devolved administration had been settled. Unionists also wanted to meet the Dublin government only as part of a larger United Kingdom delegation. The SDLP thought that unionists should meet Dublin in their own right.

The significance is plain. Brooke's initiative ran into problems because although there appeared to be willingness on all sides to talk there was no agreement as to what should be talked about. Central to the unionist agenda was devolution. Central to the nationalist agenda was the Anglo-Irish Agreement. Unionists wished to see the Agreement ended, nationalists to see it 'transcended'. The 'talks about talks' were unlikely to bear fruit unless this could be resolved.

A more sceptical reading held that neither side was anxious for formal talks even to begin. Each had its reasons for inertia. The SDLP was doubtful of devolution in the first place and had the Anglo-Irish Agreement as a fall-back. Unionists had the assurance of continued direct rule. On the other hand, there was also pressure to make the talks work, especially in the unionist camp. No one wanted to be seen to have caused their failure, and it was particularly the wish of the DUP that they succeed. In this sense unionist division worked to the advantage of the initiative.

The most compelling reason to continue to talk was Brooke himself. His analysis of the Northern problem was sufficiently dextrous to allow each side to derive support for its own position. Equally, each feared that *not* to talk could swing an advantage to the other.

TALKS BEGIN: 1991

These glimmers were enough to keep the initiative alive. Recognising that greater danger lay in non-negotiation than in negotiation, the unionist leadership eventually consented to formal talks without prior ending of the Anglo-Irish Agreement. They agreed also that it would not be necessary for a devolution plan to be in place before they would meet representatives from Dublin. (The fear of the SDLP and of the Republic's government had been that talks about devolution would become bogged down, making it impossible to move beyond that stage.) Brooke was therefore able to tell the House of Commons on 26 March 1991 that talks would begin. They would consider 'three sets of relationships' – those internal to Northern Ireland, those between North and South, and those between the two parts of the island and Britain – and would take place in three strands corresponding to each relationship. The aim would be to achieve a 'new and more broadly based agreement to give adequate expression to the totality of the relationships'.

If congratulation was in order, so too was caution. Procedural matters (the venue for the talks, the chairman) had yet to be settled, and their resolution lent a note almost of comedy to the following months. It was finally agreed that the talks would be held at Stormont, that 'strand one' would be chaired by the Secretary of State and 'strand two' by Sir Ninian Stephen, former Governor-General of Australia.

The talks proper began in June 1991 – a year and a half after Brooke had launched his initiative. Almost as soon as they started, the talks were over. The unionists withdrew because a scheduled meeting of the Anglo-Irish conference was not cancelled to enable the 'strand one' process to continue. Thus a courtship of 18 months produced a marriage which lasted three weeks. Brooke was 'naturally disappointed' but, ever the optimist, argued that 'foundations have been laid for progress in the future which neither cynics nor the men of violence will be able to undermine'. Others were less sanguine.

TALKS RESUME: 1992

The proximity of the British general election, especially one of uncertain outcome, made further progress unlikely. No party was prepared to take a position which would leave it exposed in the event of a change of administration. By the same token, the Conservative victory in April 1992 made resumption of talks highly probable because government policy was now fixed for some years to come, and parties would find it difficult to think of excuses for silence. When Sir Patrick Mayhew replaced Peter Brooke at the Northern Ireland Office, political dialogue was quickly resumed. It was as if a speedy resumption could cover collective embarrassment at the previous speedy collapse.

This second effort fared better than the first. The talks lasted half a year – achievement in itself – and although they ended acrimoniously some progress was recorded. If nothing else, symbolic victories were won. A ministerial delegation from Dublin met unionist leaders in July 1992, the first time that had happened since Sunningdale in 1973. Ulster Unionists also travelled to Dublin regularly, though the Democratic Unionists declined the opportunity. These may have appeared slender gestures, but they counted for much. For a time it seemed as if good will alone might generate real change.

The optimism was overdone. Matters of substance were discussed, but ultimately two issues could not be resolved. Unionists wanted to see an end to Dublin's territorial claim to Northern Ireland. Dublin declined. For their part, Dublin and the SDLP wanted to see a greater role for the Republic in the governance of Northern Ireland. The unionists declined. For all the effort, there was little to show. Familiar arguments were repeated, leading each side to question the seriousness of purpose of the others. If the anti-climactic talks of June 1991 seemed a comedy of errors, the lengthier dialogue of April to November 1992 looked like much ado about nothing.

Why the failure? At bottom lay disagreement about Northern Ireland's constitutional status as part of the United Kingdom. This, to the two unionist parties, was non-negotiable. Without 'open and unambiguous acknowledgement' of it, the talks could not proceed. To the SDLP and the Irish government, however, it was precisely the question of status which required most serious attention. Borrowing from a Heath administration White Paper of 1973, the Republic's government suggested, in its final submission to the talks, that the central problem lay in 'disagreement not just about how Northern Ireland should be governed but as to whether it should exist at all'.

For all that, the process generated important clarifications. Unionists, reluctantly accepting the logic of the Anglo-Irish Agreement and of the talks themselves, acknowledged at last the existence of an 'Irish dimension'. They proposed a threefold settlement: establishment of a council of the British Isles, consisting of the London and Dublin governments and representatives of any future devolved assembly in Northern Ireland; an inter-Irish relations committee 'which would facilitate business between the Belfast and Dublin administrations'; and participation of Northern Ireland representatives on any British-Irish interparliamentary tier.

Perhaps failure also revealed something of the futility of British rationality in the face of Irish politics. The talks assumed that goodwill alone could achieve much. They also assumed the existence of that goodwill in the first place. But there was no reason to imagine that unionists would consent to a greater role for Dublin merely because Dublin asked for such a role as it were face to face. Nor was Dublin likely to drop its territorial claim simply because unionists could demonstrate in person that they disliked it. The participants may have been talking, but they were talking at cross purposes.

Perhaps the very structure of the talks played a part in their ultimate failure. The formula that nothing would be agreed until everything was agreed merely made it likely that nothing would be agreed. This rigidity was also reflected in the formality of the sessions. Paradoxically, greater progress was made precisely as the participants became aware that the dialogue was heading towards stalemate. Mayhew noticed that in the last weeks of the talks, when informal conversations took place at Stormont in corridors, small rooms and even the bar, 'people got on better'. That was the sort of environment, he said, 'where the horses are bought and sold ... and horses were being bought and sold these past four weeks'.[1] This was necessary optimism, designed to keep alive the possibility of later resumption. For all that, it gave a glimpse of what might have been.

DEALING WITH MAJOR: 1993

Politics in Northern Ireland took a different turn in 1993, though in some ways it was in fact all too familiar. Just as in March 1979 the minority Labour government led by James Callaghan had sought Ulster Unionist support when faced with a vote of confidence (which in the event it lost), so in July 1993 the Conservative government led by John Major turned to OUP-leader James Molyneaux for support when the contentious Maastricht Treaty reached its final parliamentary hurdle. The difference in 1993 was that Major led a majority government which faced defeat at the hands of its own rebellious backbenchers – and that he himself tabled a motion of confidence as a means of forcing them into line.

For the Ulster Unionists it was an ideal opportunity to rebuild links with the Conservative – and Unionist (as Major took to reminding them) – Party. A Labour Party discussion document, released by

Northern Ireland spokesman Kevin McNamara at the start of July 1993, had already provoked similar reactions from leaders of the two parties. Its central proposal – imposition of joint Anglo-Irish sovereignty on Northern Ireland – was naturally anathema to Ulster Unionists. For Major, it provided a welcome chance to play the Union card. A beleaguered prime minister who had used a similar tactic to great effect when faced with the question of Scottish independence in the closing days of the 1992 general election campaign was not likely to pass it up.

Both parties were naturally coy about the terms of their parliamentary understanding. 'Nothing was asked for, nothing was offered, nothing was given' was Major's response to Seamus Mallon's allegation of 'sordid deals'. However, as the *Economist* noted, the price paid for nine Ulster Unionist votes seemed to have three main components.[2] The first was increased regional aid for Northern Ireland. Here Major was fortunate in having £2 billion of EC money to distribute between Northern Ireland, Merseyside and the Scottish Highlands. When actual distributions were announced Ulster did indeed seem to have gained at the expense of the other two deprived regions. The second was a Commons select committee on Northern Ireland, unpopular with nationalists who dislike any extension of Westminster's competence to deal with Irish affairs, but popular with unionists who believe that Ulster suffers from a 'democratic deficit'. The third was devolution of a few extra powers to local councils in Northern Ireland, possibly linked to extension of the power-sharing experiments which have been launched in a number of towns and cities in the province.

One important casualty of the new understanding between the Conservatives and the Ulster Unionists could be the long process of talks sponsored by Brooke and Mayhew, due for resumption in autumn 1993. Talks between John Hume, leader of the nationalist SDLP, and Gerry Adams, leader of Sinn Fein, in early summer 1993 were thought by some to be the prelude to genuinely all-party talks on the future of Northern Ireland. However, the Major-Molyneaux deal could make the Conservative government extremely reluctant to do anything that might offend Ulster Unionists. In these circumstances, nationalists may conclude that further talks would be a waste of time. These problems notwithstanding, the official line promulgated by Mayhew expresses hope that the programme of discussion will continue. If so, their balance shall have altered.

BRITISH POLICY IN PERSPECTIVE

When the talking and dealing were over, where stood British policy? Mayhew provided an important statement of it in December 1992 when he reaffirmed the government's commitment to dialogue and its own neutrality in that dialogue. Considered dispassionately, the events of July 1993 did not materially alter the government's stance. There was, Mayhew said, no British 'blueprint' for Northern Ireland, save to facilitate the constitutional wishes of its people. If the majority wished to remain within the United Kingdom, so be it. If in the future the majority were to wish to enter a United Ireland, the government would place no obstacle in its way. He continued:

> It is entirely consistent with such an ideal that the government is pledged to return as much responsibility as possible into the hands of local politicians ... No legitimate grouping [should be] excluded from a fair opportunity to share in the exercise of this responsibility ...[3]

But what constituted a legitimate grouping? Sir Patrick's definition was broad: any organisation which disavowed violence. Sinn Fein had only to distance itself from the IRA to become involved in talks:

> There are leading Sinn Fein speakers who voice their wish for a peaceful solution and their desire to follow a constitutional path. Provided it is advocated constitutionally, there can be no proper reason for excluding any political objective from discussion ...

Continuing the note of reconciliation, Sir Patrick acknowledged that Britain's role in the history of Ireland had not always been 'uplifting'. He conceded also that, the best efforts of recent years notwithstanding, the burden of economic disadvantage still rested more heavily on the Catholic than the Protestant population.

A hint of disengagement could be detected in the speech. As with Brooke's first forays, its purpose was to involve Sinn Fein in talks by making it possible for it to renounce 'armed struggle' with-out loss of face. Reaction was predictable. With characteristic delicacy, Ian Paisley called it a 'wicked' speech by a 'wicked Secretary of State'. Peter Robinson denounced the policy of 'surrender'.[4] More temperately, Ulster Unionists welcomed Mayhew's call for an end to violence but – missing his logic and supplying some of their own – urged selective internment to that end. The SDLP gave the policy broad support.

The most important reaction was also the most instructive. Sinn Fein was initially dismissive of the claim that Britain lacked a blueprint for Northern Ireland. The blueprint, argued Gerry Adams, was continued partition and occupation, the evidence of it every soldier in the streets of Belfast and Derry. On the other hand, there were signs that Adams, too, recognised the overture. A week after Mayhew's speech, he replied in more emollient terms, arguing that Sinn Fein had an electoral mandate to sit at any talks and that the European Community might have a role to play in brokering a settlement. These were, on each side, tentative gestures. Their initial product was SDLP-Sinn Fein talks in early summer 1993.

Less tentative, indeed alarmingly frank, was an interview given by Mayhew to *Die Zeit*, a German newspaper, in April 1993. Rehearsing the familiar argument that Britain had no strategic interest in remaining in Northern Ireland, and substantial financial interest in removing itself, Sir Patrick seemed to confirm unionist fears of betrayal. A slip of the tongue revealed much:

> Many people believe that we would not want to release Northern Ireland from the United Kingdom. To be entirely honest, we would, with pleasure. No, not with pleasure, I take that back. But we would not stand in the way of Northern Ireland if that would be the will of the majority ...

Sinn Fein could hardly have wished for a broader hint that the path of renunciation and negotiation lay open to it. Nor could unionists mistake the note of profound impatience with a policy of permanent intransigence.

NOTES

1 *Irish Times*, 17 November 1992.
2 *Economist*, 31 July 1993, p.33.
3 *Irish Times*, 17 December 1992.
4 Ibid.

CONCLUSION

Whenever the English think they have solved the Irish question, the Irish change the question. So runs one interpretation of this seemingly endless conflict, and perhaps it is not as flippant as it may first appear. Think of the various 'solutions' proposed or enacted during the nineteenth century alone: the Act of Union, Catholic Emancipation, repeal of the union, Church reform, land reform, Home Rule, 'Constructive Unionism', law and order. No sooner was one attempted than another was needed, as if the symptoms of an illness were being treated but not the illness itself. Or think of this century. After a rebellion, a war of independence, partition, a civil war, self-government, a civil rights movement, and 25 years of variously managed 'troubles', one part of Ireland remains as far from stability as ever. Politicians, paramilitaries, churchmen, foreign governments, peace movements, academics, ordinary citizens, have offered assorted solutions. None has worked. The patient, it seems, is being diagnosed to death.

QUESTIONS ABOUT QUESTIONS

Much depends on asking the right question. Should we, for instance, speak of the 'Irish problem' or the 'Northern Irish problem'? Of the 'Ulster problem' or the 'English problem'? These are not trivial distinctions. A solution satisfactory to one party shall be unsatisfactory to another if each seeks remedy for a different difficulty.

Indeed the history of the conflict since the signing of the Anglo-Irish Agreement (if not a good deal before) has been the history not of finding answers but of attempting to agree on the question. Unionists opposed 'Hillsborough' not so much because it gave the Republic a say in the running of Northern Ireland – very little say, if truth be told – but because they denied that Northern Ireland's affairs were any of the Republic's business in the first place.

Likewise the Brooke-Mayhew talks. To outsiders it seems perverse that 'talks about talks' should have lasted far longer than the talks themselves. But that was probably how it should have been. Establishing ground-rules meant establishing a question to be answered. It meant the acknowledgement of claims. Consider how procedure and agenda may become freighted with significance. To hold talks at Stormont implied the primacy of an 'internal' solution. To hold them under the neutral chairmanship of the Secretary of State implied British agnosticism about the outcome. To hold 'strand two' – meetings between the Northern Ireland parties and the Republic's government – before a devolved administration had been settled, implied that North-South relations came first. In a strange sense, talks about talks were more important than the talks themselves, because they centred on the key difficulty: the fact that for years each party to the conflict has been reluctant to accept the legitimacy of the others' perspectives, let alone their merits.

THE RELIGIOUS DIMENSION

So is the question one of tribalism, religion, imperialism, class, discrimination, inherited enmity, or simple irrationality? In so far as the uninvolved consider the matter, it is probably to cast it in terms of Catholic versus Protestant. They may also imply, with a kind of historical fatalism, that each is doomed to fight the other – like Montagu and Capulet – from generation to generation: a feud sustained by its own memory whose origins are forgotten and irrelevant.

But this is a description, not an explanation; and not a very good description at that. Little of substance is said of the Northern Ireland conflict by the claim that Catholics and Protestants find themselves on opposing sides of it. Sectarianism, it is true, has played a part. Men have been killed because of religion. Men have killed because of it. But what is being fought for is not religious hegemony.

Besides, other indicators suggest a secondary role for doctrinal differences. In the first place, most Catholics *qua* Catholics, Protestants *qua* Protestants, are repelled by continuing violence. In the second place, church leaders – Catholic, Church of Ireland, Presbyterian, Methodist – have unitedly and consistently condemned paramilitarism. In the third place, the Provisional IRA is palpably anti-Catholic in ethos. It represents an alternative source of authority to that of the Church, and no love is lost between the two. It makes no claim to be fighting for a Catholic united Ireland. It does not seek and does not expect ecclesiastical sanction for its actions. The same is broadly the case with loyalist paramilitaries. Shadowy connections with some fundamentalist preachers do not constitute a Protestant crusade to convert the infidel, an evidently counter-productive exercise.

Why then the persistence of religious explanation? It is partly because, like any half-truth, it is half true. Religion narrowly defined cannot be discounted entirely as an element in the Northern Ireland problem. It is a label for something altogether deeper, but to many the label and the product are scarcely distinguishable, and to a few they have become one and the same thing.

THE CULTURAL DIMENSION

The deeper reality is this: that in Northern Ireland there exists a cultural disharmony between the majority of the population and the minority, the former seeing themselves as 'British Irish', the latter as 'Irish Irish'. Differences of denomination are a contingency of this, not an essential element; but it is a contingency so ingrained that some do not care to see beyond it.

Consider loyalism. Is Protestantism an expression of 'Britishness' or is 'Britishness' an expression of Protestantism? Some loyalists undoubtedly see the link with the crown as a guarantee of reformation principles. The Act of Succession – which prevents the heir to the throne from marrying a Catholic, and the monarch from being Catholic – has considerable appeal to Free Presbyterians. Any constitutional reform which would as it were 'deprotestantise' the monarchy would require some loyalists to reconsider their loyalty. On the other hand there are some unionists for whom 'Britishness' implies religious toleration. The 1689 settlement, they claim, guaranteed freedom of religion within the framework of established Anglicanism. (Historically it is a difficult brief to argue.) The link with the crown is not, therefore, a guarantee of their Protestantism so much as a guarantee that they shall not be swamped by the Catholicism of a united Ireland. In both instances there is a sense that religion and the 'British way of life' are closely but not interchangeably connected.

Consider also nationalism. Irish patriotism has never been the property of one creed – witness Protestants such as Tone, Emmett, Butt, Parnell, Douglas Hyde, for whom love of country implied no sectarian exclusivity. But the ethos of the Irish Republic remains, even in a pluralist age, largely Catholic. There are historical reasons for this, dating from at least the late seventeenth century. O'Connell's mass movement nationalism in the early nineteenth century cemented the relationship between priests and people in Ireland. Patrick Pearse saw Gaelic nationhood in romantically not to say luridly Catholic terms.

More recently, the Republic's 1937 Constitution, while not establishing Catholicism as the state religion, recognises its special place in Irish life. (The Constitution also reflects Catholic social teaching in certain areas, such as the family and possession of private property.) Bishops, not politicians or newspaper editors, shape moral sentiment. Most politicians are Catholic. Political parties raise funds at church gates. The Republic has become self-consciously pluralist in the last 25 years, but social attitudes to divorce, abortion and contraception remain more conservative than in almost any other European country. A first-time visitor shall notice jarring contrasts: the Americanisation of the capital (Madonna and McDonald's) and the wayside shrines of the countryside (Madonna and child); a pause for Catholic prayer on state-run television service followed by the latest news from Hollywood. But even as the Catholic Church's grip weakens, it remains the strongest cultural force in the country.

And so, if Irish nationalism in its simplest sense means reunification of the 'national' territory, it means that Northern Ireland would become part of what appears to many Protestants to be a semi-confessional state, a fact few southerners recognise.

NORTHERN POLITICS OF NEGATION

This may be the nub of the matter. If there has been a consistent theme in Northern Irish life since the creation of the state, it is unionist resistance to any association with the south. A politics of negation existed from the start. During the Stormont years, loyalist identity depended on a series of nots: not like the south in culture or character, in language or literature, in faith or feeling; nor like the south (to be more practical) in economic performance or social provision. Perhaps Lord Craigavon spoke more truly than he realised in 1934. Here indeed was a protestant parliament, a protestant people: a people protesting their distinctiveness, their northernness, their desire to be apart.

Was this, as a matter of popular culture, an assertion of Britishness? To some extent, yes. What after all constituted Britishness for unionists but a set of emblems and attitudes – keeping souvenirs of royal visits, tuning in to the Home Service, following county cricket, standing for an anthem? But even more was it an assertion of 'Ulsterness'; that sense that, on the island of Ireland, there was no single Irish identity but several. Here, however, the iconography was not always benign. The Irish version of Britishness lacked gentility: the thrash of the lambeg drum on Orange marches, 'God Bless King Billy', 'No Pope here'. 'Ulster' may stand for hardy virtues – self-reliance, individualism, plain-speech, frugality – but when it became politicised it too often atrophied into wilfulness and intolerance.

Tutored in such a school, it is no surprise that unionists reacted with alarm to any sign of North-South *rapprochement*: the O'Neill-Lemass talks, the Council of Ireland, the Anglo-Irish Agreement. For them there could be no middle way. If unionism derived much of its legitimacy from a northerly contradistinction, then amity with the south was the first step towards amalgamation. Ulster had to keep its distance or disappear.

SOUTHERN POLITICS OF IMMATURITY

The southern Irish state's territorial claim over Northern Ireland lent plausibility to the fear. Yet how serious was that claim? How serious is it now? It was sufficiently serious in the earliest years of the state to result in civil war. That war defined the framework of Irish politics for decades thereafter. From opposing sides emerged the two main parties of the state – Fianna Fail, Fine Gael – which are only now being challenged for electoral hegemony by secular, progressive groups. Fianna Fail, creation of Eamon de Valera, comprised those who had opposed the 1921 treaty which partitioned Ireland; Fine Gael, those who had accepted it as the best available interim settlement.

Each considered reunification to be desirable , but Fianna Fail gave the impression that it was a priority. In reality it was no such thing. After the report of the Boundary Commission in 1925 the border became a secondary issue in Irish politics: a rhetorical device at election times, little more. There was no immediate prospect of the re-integration of the 'national territory', and no need, therefore, to defer more pressing matters in its favour.

The effect on Irish national life was not entirely healthy. In odd ways, southern nationalists needed the north just as northern unionists needed the south. The existence of each validated the other in its sense of historical grievance. Just as unionism soured into bigotry, so nationalism had a tendency to sour into anti-Britishness. The notion of a revolution not quite complete but unable to be completed pervaded Irish life, causing a kind of political stuntedness or immaturity. When things went wrong it was easier to blame a 'continued British presence' than to solve the problems. The northern state, and unionists in particular, served useful demonological purposes. It helped, of course, that unionists were, indeed, poor custodians of democracy.

Many southerners knew little of 'the North'; never visited it; considered its inhabitants (even nationalists) different from themselves. It had minimal significance in their lives. The sentimentalities of nationalism were of course accorded due respect – in pub and song if not in practical politics. The 'Black North' work so well as myth that no one dared devote much time to the reality.

At the beginning of the 'troubles' there was genuine sympathy for the plight of the minority. A vague solicitude remains. The chief disposition of public opinion, however, appears to be bafflement at the longevity of the conflict combined with a desire to have as little as possible to do with it. The North is a fearful embarrassment to the South; a financial drain (in terms of security and lost revenue); a cause of political destabilisation; a monumental distraction. The idea of assuming responsibility for it fills most citizens of the Irish Republic with dread.

BRITISH INTERESTS

And Britain? The notion that part of Ireland is occupied against its will by an imperialist power should now be recognised as simple-minded. It should be equally clear that Britain has little interest, financial or strategic, in remaining in Northern Ireland. If any will is being flouted by Britain's presence it is Britain's. The costs are enormous and rising; the bar of world opinion is generally unfavourable; terrorism has been introduced to the streets of London and elsewhere; the prime minister and cabinet were once nearly eliminated *en masse*; soldiers are regularly returned home in boxes. Britain stays not because it wishes to, but because it cannot in good conscience withdraw. If the solution were that simple, we can be sure that the problem would have been solved long ago.

The irony should not be lost. Unionists are busy resisting integration into a state which has no practical desire to integrate them. (Naturally, if they did not resist, the desire might return.) Meantime nationalists are fighting (by whatever means) to enter a polity which on the whole would rather not have them. Britain looks on, part of the problem according to one side, part of the solution according to the other. (The sides in question may be filled in according to taste.)

FUTURE PROSPECTS

Common sense suggests that this is an argument for splitting the difference: for allowing Northern Ireland its separate status, with power-sharing to keep the minority sweet. But that would mean the victory of one 'tradition' over another, and this would never do. In Ireland, 'face' is important. What matters is not that nationalism or unionism be ultimately victorious – it is hard to imagine how this could happen – but that each be deemed to be a legitimate tradition, worthy of respect by the other. Consider Irish Minister for Foreign Affairs Dick Spring in March 1993:

> Our problem stems essentially from opposing fears that the members of one or other tradition will be the ultimate minority, and therefore, it is assumed, the ultimate losers in an immemorial historical conflict ... We must recognise that there can be no lasting peace and stability in Ireland unless and until the two main traditions on the island cooperate ...

Unfortunately, as one tradition necessarily excludes the other, the politics of legitimacy are also the politics of perpetual instability; perhaps also, if Spring be typical, of perpetual platitude.

It is ambitious, then, to speak of a solution to the problem when the problem itself is so elusive of definition. Each side has certainly solved *some* problem to its own satisfaction. The trick is to get each to solve the *same* problem.

How to do this? Perhaps by the creation of a new political language. It has been said that what Catholics and Protestants need in Northern

Ireland is a common enemy. That after all is how other societies get on. But the polite fictions by which other places live – that 'inflation is public enemy number one', or Communism, or unemployment, or 'the deficit' – are too polite for Northern Ireland. There is an elemental quality to the struggle which refuses to be civilised by language or smoothed away by euphemism. Even to talk of 'traditions' is to conceal a multitude of enmities, some imagined, some real, some no less real for being imagined. Ulster, it seems, is still a place apart, and likely to remain so for some time to come.

APPENDICES

Appendix 1 Prime Ministers of Northern Ireland, 1921-72

Sir James Craig, Lord Craigavon 1921-40
John Miller Andrews 1940-43
Sir Basil Brooke, Lord Brookeborough 1943-63
Captain Terence O'Neill 1963-69
Major James Chichester-Clark 1969-71
Brian Faulkner 1971-72

Appendix 2 Secretaries of State for Northern Ireland, 1972-93

William Whitelaw (C) 1972-73
Francis Pym (C) 1973-74
Merlyn Rees (L) 1974-76
Roy Mason (L) 1976-79
Humphrey Atkins (C) 1979-81
James Prior (C) 1981-84
Douglas Hurd (C) 1984-85
Tom King (C) 1985-89
Peter Brooke (C) 1989-92
Sir Patrick Mayhew (C) 1992-

A BRIEF GUIDE TO FURTHER READING

There is now a vast and expanding literature on the Northern Ireland problem. Of particular value are:

Arthur P and K Jeffrey, *Northern Ireland since 1968* (Blackwell, Oxford, 1988)

Aughey A, *Under Siege: Ulster Unionism and the Anglo-Irish Agreement* (Hurst and Company, London, 1989)

Bishop P and E Mallie, *The Provisional IRA* (Heinemann, London, 1987)

Boyle K and T Hadden, *The Anglo-Irish Agreement: Commentary, Text and Official Review* (Sweet and Maxwell, London, 1989)

Buckland P, *A History of Northern Ireland* (Gill and Macmillan, Dublin, 1981)

Farrell M, *Northern Ireland: The Orange State* (Pluto Press, London, 1976)

Flackes W D and S Elliott, *Northern Ireland: A Political Directory 1968-1988* (Blackstaff Press, Belfast, 1989)

Gaffikin F and M Morrissey, *Northern Ireland: The Thatcher Years* (Zed Books, London, 1990)

McKittrick D, *Despatches from Belfast* (Blackstaff Press, Belfast, 1989)

Moloney E and A Pollak, *Paisley* (Poolbeg Press, Dublin, 1986)

O'Leary B and J McGarry, *The Politics of Antagonism: Understanding Northern Ireland* (Athlone Press, London, 1993)

O'Malley P, *Northern Ireland: Questions of Nuance* (Blackstaff Press, Belfast, 1990)

Stewart A T Q, *The Narrow Ground: The Roots of Conflict in Ulster* (Faber and Faber, London, 1989)

White B, *John Hume: Statesman of the Troubles* (Blackstaff, Belfast, 1984)

Whyte J H, *Interpreting Northern Ireland* (Clarendon Press, Oxford, 1990)

Wilson T, *Ulster: Conflict and Consent* (Blackwell, Oxford, 1988)

INDEX

Adams, Gerry
  Anglo-Irish Agreement 69
  unionism 89
Alliance Party
  Constitutional Convention 32
  power-sharing 29
  'rolling devolution' 35
An End to Drift 35
Anglo-Irish Agreement
  Council of Ireland 40
  Irish Constitution 40-1
  perceived failure 42
  political ambiguity 83
Atkins, Humphrey 34, 44, 46

Bates, Dawson 17
'Birmingham Six' 81
British and Irish Intergovernmental
    Council 37
Brooke, Peter
  analysis of Northern Ireland
      problem 94
  shrewdness 91
  Sinn Fein 93
Bush, George 75

Charter Group 63
Chichester-Clark, James 24-5
Clinton, Bill 75
Connolly, James 11, 13
Conservative Party
  1979 manifesto 43
  unionism 98
Constitutional Convention, 1975 32-3
Craig, James, Viscount Craigavon
    17, 19, 104
Craig, William
  Constitutional Convention 32
  political strikes 33
  Vanguard 27-8, 32

De Lorean Motor Company 55
Democratic Unionist Party (DUP)
  Anglo-Irish Agreement 41
  Atkins talks 41
  Brooke talks 94ff
  emergence 62
  rise 64
  'rolling devolution' 35, 48, 64-5

social complexion 64-5
  character 64-5

Easter Rising 13

Faulkner, Brian
  Constitutional Convention 32
  Council of Ireland 30
  Paisley 29
  power-sharing 29
  prime minister 25-6
Fenianism 9
Fitt, Gerry, Lord Fitt 30
Fitzgerald, Garrett
  Anglo-Irish Agreement 37, 83
  Thatcher 48

Gaelic Revival 11
Glorious Revolution 6
Gladstone, William Ewart 10
Grattan's Parliament 7-8
Government of Ireland Act 1920 14

Haughey, Charles 34
  Anglo-Irish Agreement 88
  anti-terrorism 86
  Thatcher 44, 46
Hume, John
  Adams 86, 99
  Anglo-Irish Agreement 41, 87-8
  Constitutional Convention 32
  EC 72-3
  fall of executive 32
  hunger strikes 45
  Mason 34
  New Ireland Forum 48
Hurd, Douglas 36, 81

Industrial Development Board (IDB) 54

King, Tom 83
  assessment of 91

Local Enterprise Development Unit
    (LEDU) 55
Lenihan, Brian 45

Mallon, Seamus 68
Mason, Roy 33-4
MacBride Principles 75
McNamara, Kevin 98
Major, John 53, 91
  Ulster Unionists and 97-8
Mayhew, Sir Patrick 91, 96
  analysis of Northern Ireland
      problem 99ff